RECLAIMING CAPITAL

Democratic Initiatives and Community Development

Christopher Gunn
Hazel Dayton Gunn

Cornell University Press
Ithaca and London

First published 1991 by Cornell University Press
First printing, Cornell Paperbacks, 1991

International Standard Book Number 0-8014-2323-6 (cloth)
International Standard Book Number 0-8014-9574-1 (paper)
Library of Congress Catalog Card Number 90-55725

Printed in the United States of America

Librarians: Library of Congress cataloging information appears on the last page of the book.

Cornell University Press strives to use environmentally responsible suppliers and materials to the fullest extent possible in the publishing of its books. Such materials include vegetable-based, low-VOC inks and acid-free papers that are recycled, totally chlorine-free, or partly composed of nonwood fibers.

Paperback printing 10 9 8 7 6 5 4 3

Contents

Preface

In the summer of 1985 we went to the Pacific Northwest to update research with the workers' cooperatives Christopher wrote about in *Workers' Self-Management in the United States* (1984). Conversations with old acquaintances and new recruits to cooperative work all turned, sooner or later, to the region's slow recovery from the Reagan-Volcker recession of 1982–83. Mill towns and major cities were in rough shape, and community activists were searching for appropriate responses. Recruit new investment, hope the economy could be diversified, try to shape local politics to help those most in need, and wait it out: these were the most common strategies. These people's sense of frustration stayed with us. As we drove east across Montana we learned that economic activity there had yet to return to the state's 1979 level. Our own discussions turned to basic questions. What made for development? What could sustain a place not favored by investment from outside? What, in a global economy, could a community do for itself?

We returned to the East and began to inquire into what was being done by professional planners, community activists, and foundation staff members. Many felt they were reacting to changes willynilly, with little sense of how to ground their efforts and formulate long-term strategy. Basic principles of radical political economy were our starting point. Social surplus could provide a conceptual framework to analyze the roots of development problems and how they might be overcome. The challenge was how to bring that abstract concept down to earth.

Our review of the academic field of development economics provided us little insight. Studies of community, local, and regional economic development and underdevelopment that we had known of a decade earlier seemed to have come to a halt. Development economics had become a specialized corner of a discipline turned inward on itself. We were looking for foundations for community-based decision making in an era in which markets were thought to reign supreme. Yes, they are important, but they also reward some communities and impoverish others. We were also reminded that development itself involved far more than economics, that political and social issues were important parts of its process.

Our work began in earnest: traditional field research on successful and unsuccessful local development projects and debate with their proponents, opponents, and doers. We studied projects, conversed with and questioned people from the Rio Grande to the St. Lawrence, and from the Northwest to North Carolina. What follows is a selective distillation of our research.

We do not argue that the world can be changed by local, small-scale activity. We offer this book in the hope that it will help guide the expenditure of progressive energy to projects that can be affected at the local level, and that it will help those engaged in this work to understand better the systemic roots of the problems they confront. From that understanding may come new forms and levels of action for social change.

Conversations with people in many walks of life and access to information in unexpected quarters fed our work on this book. We can only begin here to thank helpful individuals and institutions. Early ideas and conceptual chapters for the manuscript received important suggestions and criticism from the late Chandler Morse, professor emeritus of economics at Cornell University, and Staughton Lynd, senior attorney at Northeast Ohio Legal Services in Youngstown. Michael E. Rotkin, director of field studies for the Division of Social Sciences at the University of California, Santa Cruz, and Edward S. Greenberg, professor of political science, University of Colorado, Boulder, later read the entire manuscript, offering encouragement and suggesting improvements.

Much of our field work for this project entailed numerous discussions of local initiatives with the people making them happen. We thank them all for sharing the stories of their accomplishments and struggles with us.

Throughout work on this volume we sought out people who were critically engaged in development work itself and those who were thinking critically about goals, strategy, and the larger picture of social change in this country. We have treasured and benefited greatly from our discussions, some brief and some long, with them. These stimulating and unusual individuals include John Gaventa, director of the Highlander Research and Education Center in New Market, Tennessee; Barry Passett, president of the Greater Southeast Community Hospital Foundation in Washington, D.C.; Roxanne Ward Zaghab, formerly of the National Center for Policy Alternatives in Washington, D.C.; Michael Freedland of the Corporation for Enterprise Development in Washington, D.C.; and Peggy Curran, director of community and economic development in Santa Monica, California. Regardless of their very different activities, these are people who wed theory and practice in innovative and inspiring ways.

Two friends agreed to read and comment on draft portions of this manuscript, and we thank them for their time, patience, and insight. They are William W. Goldsmith of the Department of City and Regional Planning at Cornell, and Richard Schramm of the Urban Studies and Planning Department at the Massachusetts Institute of Technology.

Hobart and William Smith Colleges provided support for several summers of travel and manuscript preparation, for which we were always grateful. Christopher's colleagues in the economics department put up with an occasionally preoccupied Chair with understanding and good cheer.

Last, we must thank the people with whom we have worked at Cornell University Press. Peter Agree provided encouragement for this project from early in its development and wise council as it took shape. Thanks also to Joanne Hindman, copy editor for this book.

HAZEL DAYTON GUNN
CHRISTOPHER GUNN

Trumansburg, New York

Reclaiming Capital

I

Social Surplus

This book offers a different way of understanding communities and their development in the United States. Our work is based on premises that the economic and the political development of communities are closely interwoven and that choices about how communities will develop are fundamentally political choices. In this sense, our subject is the political economy of communities.[1]

Communities are understood here as locationally defined groups of people who have some common characteristics, such as the kind of work they do or their racial or ethnic background, and some common interests resulting from their proximity, such as levels of public services or concern for the environment in which they live.[2]

[1] "Political economy" is a term of varied usage. We use it to mean a study that is interdisciplinary in nature, one that pays close attention to economic, political, and social institutions and relations and the outcomes of activities in those realms. Rather than looking to individuals or nations as principal actors, it investigates the action of groups that are defined by their common interests in society, interests derived from within the system itself. Political economy recognizes conflict as inherent among those groups in capitalist society; the metaphor of the invisible hand offers little insight. Change is taken to be constant in life. See "The Resurgence of Political Economy" in the introductory section of *Alternatives to Economic Orthodoxy: A Reader in Political Economy*, ed. Randy Albelda, Christopher Gunn, and William Waller (Armonk, N.Y., 1987).

[2] The literature on communities is extensive and diverse. A recent summary of its more sociological segment can be found in Albert Hunter and Suzanne Staggenborg, "Local Communities and Organized Action," in *Community Organizations: Studies in Resource Mobilization and Exchange*, ed. Carl Milofsky (New York, 1988), pp. 243–76. Both political arguments and class-based aspects of the literature are summarized in the first two chapters of Ira Katznelson, *City Trenches: Urban Politics and the Patterning of Class in the United States* (New York, 1981). The introductory chapters of Barry Bluestone and

People who share a sense of community can do things together. They can also divide and fight. We hold no romantic notions of either contemporary, bygone, or future communitarian utopias. Evidence of less cohesive outcomes such as racism surrounds us routinely.

Capital is conceptually distinct from communities. It can be understood as both financial wherewithal for economic development and as a group in society that controls economic resources and shares an interest in perpetuating control over them. Capital wants profit; communities want development. Communities want well-paying jobs for their residents; investors are driven to pay the lowest possible wages relative to capital costs at given levels of productivity. Capital seeks an environment free of costly regulation; communities require a life-sustaining ecology. Communities are defined by place and stability; capital is concerned with location primarily as a factor in transportation and transaction costs. These are some of the major issues over which confrontation occurs between capital and communities.[3]

We set out to learn how communities confront capital in the United States; we found that they do so on their knees. Our aim is to identify clearly how people acting together as citizens can gain greater control over their lives—over the present and future development of their communities. Focusing analysis on the concept of social surplus and its creation, appropriation, and end use, we explore the current relationship between communities and capital. In the process we investigate ways of modifying the unequal relationship between them and ultimately argue for changing the nature of that relationship.

We will not argue that community-based activity is *the* answer to bringing about social change. It is one of many. The community shares some characteristics and scale with schools and the workplace, and, if you stretch a bit, even the household. Spatially and politically, communities are intertwined with state, regional, national, and global systems, institutions, and directions of change. Complex societies cannot be neatly disassembled for action any more than for analysis, and we have simply chosen communities as an entry point to highlight locally based action for social change.

Bennett Harrison, *The Deindustrialization of America* (New York, 1982), enumerate economic elements of the literature.

[3] Chapter 1 of Bluestone and Harrison, *Deindustrialization of America*, provides evidence of some of the ways these contradictions have affected communities that have lost major employers.

Why Social Surplus?

Life in a particular society and era carries with it a basic understanding of how the world works, an understanding that includes a mix of thought and conjecture about much that we do not comprehend well. Explanations of how and why development takes place give communities little sense of how to initiate development that they can control. We suggest what will be, for most readers, a different way to make sense of how the world works and of the development process. The effort required to make this conceptual shift is justified, we believe, by its result—a clearer grasp of the challenge facing communities seeking their own paths to development today.

In response to the need for a more critical and substantial conceptual framework to guide analysis of local and regional economies, we provide a sketch of an alternative that will require years of shared development and refinement. We believe that the study of community economic development badly needs debate over fundamentals rather than timid tinkering. Our approach is controversial because it promotes an expansion of public planning and of citizen participation in the planning process. It is also based on the idea that planning is often futile without resources to implement desired outcomes. We identify institutions—now small in number and limited in use—that place expanded amounts of resources under democratic control, and we call them alternative institutions of accumulation. They provide alternatives, of course, to traditional corporations and private decision making. If democratic control of society is to be expanded, development of these and new, unforeseen alternatives to existing ways of both producing and controlling social surplus is essential.

Any society that is developed beyond an ability to produce only enough to keep it at a subsistence level from one period to the next generates social surplus. Social surplus is the difference between the net product of a society and the consumption (in individual and collective forms) that is essential to maintain those who do the producing. Some portion of the surplus can then be used to raise the productive capability of society in the future. Examples of the use of surplus in agricultural production have included drying and storing the best grains of a harvest to assure more or better quality seed for next season's planting, or using part of the revenue of goods sold at market to purchase a draft animal so that in coming years more goods could be produced. Industrial corporations today devote a portion of their income to researching new and more efficient ways of producing and then developing the most promising of them. Governments tax away a portion of surplus and use it to fund improved education or transportation infrastructure. In all these examples, specific gains in efficiency—gains in output relative to units of resources used in production—combine in a historical trend toward higher levels of human productiveness, a principle that has been at the heart of economic development.

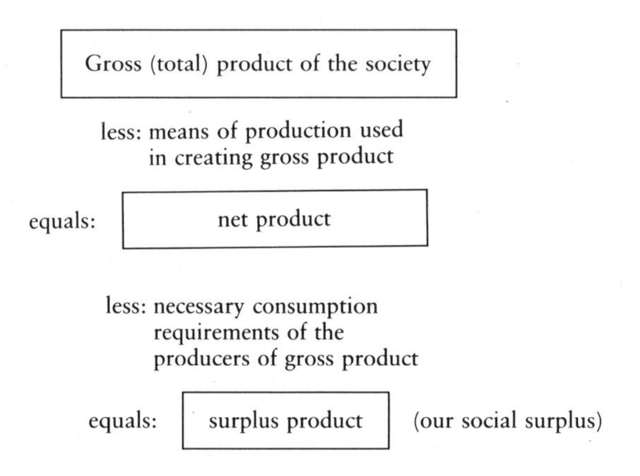

Through invention of and investment in better tools and equipment and through education and skills development for people who will work with that equipment and improve it further, society gains the ability to produce more surplus. Development is reflected in rising product per capita—a realization of the expectation of more tomorrow than today. Although in many contemporary societies "more" is thought of in terms of more income with which to buy more privately consumed goods, other options are possible. A society may choose a higher level of services for individuals or households, or more collectively consumed goods or services such as healthcare or cultural activities. Or it may resolve to work less the next year, consuming all or part of its augmented surplus in the form of more leisure time.

What happens to social surplus in capitalist societies? The answer is not obvious. No business or government account carries the label, yet it is clear that social surplus—huge amounts of it by historical standards—is generated around the clock in such an economy. It appears in income categories of rent to property owners and profit and interest to capital owners. It appears in use categories such as business reinvestment which account for growth rather than simple maintenance of current levels of activity. It appears as government revenue from taxes paid by businesses and individuals (assuming that nobody is taxed to a level of disposable income below the accepted level of subsistence). And among high-income segments of society, it appears in what Thorstein Veblen termed conspicuous consumption.[4]

By drawing attention to social surplus, we do not mean to argue that wage rates do not matter to a community. Higher wages may accompany conditions of production that use advanced technologies or high education and skill levels in the service sector. When higher wages have been won, workers live better lives, and the higher income is beneficial to the local economy as a basis for generating other income.

Savings are a repository of social surplus. Households and individuals save for a variety of reasons, and in doing so they create a pool of surplus from which businesses can draw funds to undertake new productive activity or from which other households or branches of government can finance current consumption. Firms also save, generally to finance future growth. In the past half century they have taken over much of the saving function that households used to perform in the U.S. economy. A century ago savings may have been lodged in a local bank where they provided a basis for further economic activity locally or regionally. Today, even if placed in a local bank, they quickly become part of an international pool; they are collected in one of a few financial centers and lent or invested worldwide. Communities no longer have to generate their own financial resources for development, but on the other hand, they may lose access to resources generated locally. What matters is the net flow. That, as we will explain, depends on a community's ability to attract private investment funds.

Social surplus is a broad term for what is also known as surplus product, or surplus value. By calling surplus "social," we hope to raise questions in readers' minds about how surplus is created, appropriated, and distributed under various economic systems and in specific communities within them. The conceptual category of social surplus is generally applied at broad levels of social and economic aggrega-

[4] Thorstein Veblen, *The Theory of the Leisure Class* (New York, 1899). In this and later writing Veblen provides a sharp and acerbic characterization of emulation patterns in consumption. His respect for those who produce in society (workers, engineers), in contrast with a growing group of wealthy consumers, is also reflected in his understanding of purely pecuniary versus substantive practices in industry. On this, see his *Instinct of Workmanship* (New York, 1914).

tion.[5] Using it in analyzing economic activity of smaller territorial and juristic levels can shed light on the development challenges they face.

Problems Communities Face

The motive force behind capitalism is incentive for private gain. In Adam Smith's well-known metaphor of the invisible hand, some benevolent force guides a system, which is based on a seemingly conflict-ridden quest for individual gratification, to yield social harmony and good. By freeing people to pursue their own self-interest through markets, material and human resources are employed in the most productive ways. The private quest to maximize profit is seen as the path to maximizing surplus produced by the system.[6] Attendant gains in productivity translate into development.

Since our concern lies with development problems facing communities in the United States today, we focus our discussion on cap-

[5] John G. Gurley, "Marx and the Critique of Capitalism," in part 4 of *Alternatives to Economic Orthodoxy*, ed. Albelda, Gunn, and Waller, provides a brief introduction. For more thorough contemporary treatment, see Duncan Foley, *Understanding Capital: Marx's Economic Theory* (Cambridge, Mass., 1986). Contemporary application of Marxist theory to urban and community issues, and some of the debates engendered in its use, are presented in the essays included in William K. Tabb and Larry Sawers, eds., *Marxism and the Metropolis*, 2d ed. (New York, 1984). David Harvey presents a contemporary restatement of Marx's theory with attention to spatial and geographical issues in his *Limits to Capital* (Chicago, 1982), and *The Urbanization of Capital: Studies in the History and Theory of Capitalist Urbanization* (Baltimore, Md., 1985). Related work can be found in the extensive writing of Manuel Castells, including *The Urban Question: A Marxist Approach* (Cambridge, Mass., 1977), *City, Class, and Power* (New York, 1979), and *The City and the Grassroots* (Berkeley, Calif., 1983). Analysis of a local economy using a Marxist framework can be found in David B. Houston, "A History of Capital Accumulation in Pittsburgh: A Marxist Interpretation," *Review of Regional Studies* 9:1 (1982), 12–22, 9:3 (1982), 81–97, and 10:2 (1983), 20–37.

[6] Existing forms of socialism, most of them highly statist in character, have attempted more direct action for development. Social surplus is aggregated at the level of the state, where rational planning can allocate it in ways deemed most essential to further production. Means of production are typically state property; they are the result of the work and sacrifices in consumption by previous generations. By restricting or eliminating private income based on property ownership, a smaller proportion of social surplus is consumed, and more is available for financing new increases in productivity and output. An ethic of work for the good of society is fostered through economic, social, and cultural emphasis on solidarity and equality. As in capitalism, social surplus makes development possible. In contrast to earlier ways of provisioning societies, both are broadly and deeply inculcated with definitions of growth and development that have a material basis.

italism in a moderately constrained market form.[7] The basic operation of the system is clear. Communities must make decisions that will enhance their attractiveness to capital, whether it is available locally or not. They have no hold on local capital. It is privately controlled, and it may or may not be locally invested at the choice of its owner. Widely advertised financial institutions point investors to national and international alternatives. Local offices of national investment firms, their toll-free telephone lines, and local banks and insurance brokers provide access to nonlocal outlets for investment. Local origin provides advantage only if investors place their funds in a business that they will run, one close to their homes. Even that kind of local investment will take place only if conditions are right.

Communities must compete for financial resources for development from the same national and international pools of capital. What will prove attractive? If investors plan to produce goods or sell services, low wages will. But if they hope to sell the goods or services near where they are produced, a low wage structure may mean a limited market, ultimately discouraging other forms of investment. What other attractions may exist for potential investors? Lack of costly environmental controls could be one. But a community with an unhealthy or unattractive environment will discourage many people and firms from locating there and perhaps drive its citizens away. Yet another attraction for capital may be relatively low-cost transportation for inputs, finished goods, or both. Since transportation infrastructure is generally state financed, communities have historically involved themselves in political contests for favorable proximity to canals, railroads, and highways. A community may set its sights on close proximity to an interstate highway interchange. If successful, it gains advantage over others more isolated in relation to national transportation patterns, but no advantage over other communities on the same or similar interstate highways across the country.

Suppose that a community can offer capital relatively low-cost transportation linkages, a pool of low-wage labor without limiting

[7] More highly constrained or regulated forms of capitalism have been common to Western Europe during recent decades. Social democratic regimes generally constrain capital to a greater extent than the United States by, for instance, restricting its ability to drive wages down or abandoning domestic production facilities while moving capital abroad, or by assuring sufficient levels of reinvestment to maintain employment in an industry that constitutes a significant portion of the economy. In countries where this has been the case, perhaps the primary contrast to the United States has been the presence of a well-organized and politically active labor movement.

the market for the good or service to be produced, and minimal existence of or enforcement of environmental standards in a relatively unspoiled natural setting. It should attract capital. Is development assured? The answer may well be no. The capital it attracts may only take advantage of these benefits while they last, or until it finds better benefits elsewhere. Numerous communities have attracted assembly and processing facilities or resource extraction investment only to find that they do not stay long, or that they provide so low or erratic a flow of wages or other factor payments into the economy that they fail to be building blocks for further development.[8] And surplus produced in these operations can, of course, be moved elsewhere.

Public sector options present themselves, but they cannot easily escape contradictions inherent in the nature of the system. The opportunity for a community to gain advantage by proximity to an interstate highway can be especially appealing because the highway is paid for from national funds; its cost is spread across the country, not borne by the community. Amenities to attract capital that must be paid for at the local level carry the onus of local financing.[9] Local citizens accept higher taxes in the hope of a payoff, but higher tax rates for local businesses discourage investment. The countryside is littered with near-empty industrial parks created at clear cost to hopeful community residents.

From the perspective of capital and of textbook economics, the system is working properly. Producers are driven to lowest cost arrangements of production, and competition assures that consumers pay the lowest price possible for their goods and services. Citizens

[8] See Jane Jacobs's discussion of "transplant regions" in her *Cities and the Wealth of Nations: Principles of Economic Life* (New York, 1984), chap. 7. Jacobs's work highlights the protean mix of ingredients which makes for development in certain city regions. Chief among them, in her view, is import replacement. From our perspective, the heart of that important process is the ability to shift creation and appropriation of social surplus to the city region. With growth in this resource, Jacobs's other four development forces (city markets for new products, increased city jobs, productivity-increasing technology, and transplanted city work) can be unleashed in the city's immediate hinterland. Without it, those forces will not appear simultaneously, and the hinterland will remain just that. See also Gene F. Summers et al., *Industrial Invasion of Non-Metropolitan America: A Quarter Century of Experience* (New York, 1976).

[9] Robert Goodman, *The Last Entrepreneurs* (Boston, 1979), describes the $100 million in state and local costs, subsidies, and tax abatements used to lure Volkswagen into a vacant auto plant in western Pennsylvania. Production began there in 1978, and Volkswagen's German headquarters closed the operation in 1989. See also William Tabb, "A Cost-Benefit Analysis of Location Subsidies for Ghetto Neighborhoods," *Land Economics* 68 (February 1972), 45–52.

can benefit from cheaper consumer goods so long as they have sufficient income to enter the particular portion of the market and choose to purchase the goods. Whatever their past level of disposable income, they can then consume more. *Voila*! Development.

For some communities, this process bears fruit. But for many others the negative outcomes sketched above are closer to reality. Just as people are divided between those with sufficient income to enjoy the fruits of development and those who are excluded from them, so too are some communities stagnating while others are developing.

Economic vitality is only one of the determinants of a viable community, but it is a central one. A local economy in decline means shrinking funding for basic services such as hospitals, schools, roads. Accompanying population decline accelerates the downward spiral. Communities once strong in neighborhood ties, broadly participating in democratic practice, and alive with economic activity can be pitched into stagnation as a result of private decisions that allocate social surplus elsewhere. Competing nationally and internationally to present a favorable environment for capital can prove injurious to a community's health, and so can failure to do so. At the heart of the matter is the degree to which any community can control its development process. Social surplus is not readily available to communities in forms that would enable them to pursue locally based public development or to encourage "third sector" initiatives such as locally based producer and consumer cooperatives. Communities that interfere in the private allocation of capital to too great an extent create a reputation for a "bad investment climate" and face further starvation of funds for development.[10] But gaining public control over capital—taking capital from capitalism—is no easy task.

Contemporary Capitalism and Surplus Value

In emphasizing community-based and local action to gain greater democratic control over economic development, we run the risk of ignoring or deemphasizing the nature of the larger system in which

[10] A charge used against community groups or local governments that challenge traditional development strategies is that they will scare off potential investors. Community activists in San Antonio, Texas, recounted to us the chilling effect of local allegations, reported in the pages of the national business press, that they were responsible for creating conditions leading to the charge of a negative investment climate in their city.

this activity is to take place. The Greens urge people to "think globally and act locally." We want to broaden the meaning of this phrase to urge understanding of the global nature of the capitalist economic system and the way it constrains local action.

The ability to generate growth—the most clearly established accomplishment of Western industrial economies—has diminished. Very moderate average growth rates of 2–3 percent per annum in gross national product, both in market-oriented versions of the system and its more constrained social democratic forms, indicate a system that has, at best, matured. And for the economy of the United States especially, even this growth rate has been achieved over a mountain of consumer, business, and government debt. Dynamic economies grow at two to three times that rate. Slow growth for the most prosperous economies has advantages: It may slow environmental degradation and it could diminish Western control over markets, perhaps allowing other countries greater opportunity to expand into the global economy.[11] It does, however, call into question one of the brightest stars in the firmament of capitalism relative to other ways of organizing economic activities.

Other contemporary problems of the system are well known. Failure to meet basic human needs—food, clothing, shelter, medical care—in societies as "developed" as Western industrial nations, as wealthy as the United States, point to the paradoxical content of the term. Surely growth, even when it was achieved more rapidly, did not necessarily lead to development. Just as surely, simple confiscation from the wealthy and redistribution to the poor would not solve these problems, although it could be important materially and symbolically. New understanding of what development means must emerge with new forms of sustainable, nonhazardous economic growth, with more even geographic and demographic distribution of its fruits, and with greater emphasis on quality of life experiences rather than quantity of material production. Can these changes occur under this economic system?

Few Americans who wrestle with these issues routinely refer to capitalists as a class or use the term "capital" to refer to that class.[12]

[11] Even when it occurs, this expansion is limited to a few countries. In the 1980s five or six "newly industrialized countries" in general authoritarian havens for transnational capital, such as South Korea, experienced real growth. For a majority of countries in the Third World, the decade of the 1980s was one of decline.

[12] "Capital" is most commonly used in the contemporary United States to refer to finance

Both descriptions can be useful. By class we do not have in mind the typical stratification categories of most contemporary social scientists in this country—middle class, upper middle class—based on household income. We adopt the more radical use of the term, which derives from careful scrutiny of the regular source of an individual's or household's income, particularly whether it results primarily from work (wages or salaries) or from property ownership (rent, interest, dividends, capital gains). If the source is property ownership, the label "capitalist class" is appropriate. Late twentieth-century American life obscures these distinctions; according to mainstream ideology they are considered too political or even un-American. In practical terms a "professional-managerial class" constitutes a large group that is difficult to locate in the traditional two-class abstraction of capital and labor.[13] Despite these difficulties, identifying the group in society which we call capital is not difficult. One shorthand method is to inspect wealth-holding in this country.

Wealth is essentially income-producing property.[14] The most ac-

---

capital, to relatively liquid assets, and as a general term for the equipment and machinery of production. A more complex use of the term occurs in Marxist analysis in which it has these meanings plus those of the capitalist class and the social relations particular to the capitalist mode of production. "Class" itself is a term fraught with complex meaning in this analysis. The class character of life includes elements on a continuum between material conditions of being and consciousness on the one hand, and on a continuum between the structure of a way of organizing material life (such as capitalism) and its routine processes and experiences on the other. For a discussion that draws on the work of the British historian E. P. Thompson to capture much of the richness of this term, see Katznelson, *City Trenches*, chap. 9.

[13] The term "professional-managerial class" is that of Barbara Ehrenreich and John Ehrenreich. See their "Professional-Managerial Class," *Radical America* 11:2 (1977), 7–31. This essay and responses to it appear in Pat Walker, ed., *Between Labor and Capital* (Boston, 1979). Whether this is a class that acts cohesively in its own interest is open to question, but it is an identifiable and growing group in the United States. Erik Wright refers to this group and some others in modern capitalist societies as in "contradictory class locations" between the interests of capital and labor. See his "Varieties of Marxist Conceptions of Class Structure," *Politics and Society* 9:3 (1980), 323–70, and *Class, Crisis and the State* (London, 1978). Wright, *Classes* (London, 1985), extends class analysis based on a rational choice model and a different definition of exploitation. See Wright et al., *The Debate on Classes* (London, 1989), for contrasting arguments on class-based analysis.

[14] An important distinction can be made between what Edward Wolfe describes as "life-cycle wealth" (equity held in the form of owner-occupied housing, durables, household inventories, demand deposits and currency, and the cash value of life insurance and pensions, all less consumer debt) and "capital wealth" (the sum of time and savings deposits, bonds and securities, corporate stock, business and investment real estate equity, and trust-fund equity). Capital wealth is dramatically less equally distributed than life-cycle wealth. Wolfe sees life-cycle wealth as accumulated for household use (housing, liquidity, and

curate recent data available indicate that in 1983 the wealthiest half of 1 percent (0.5 percent) of families in the United States owned 26.9 percent of all personal wealth. When personal residences are excluded, their percentage of wealth is considerably higher. The same half of 1 percent owns 46.5 percent of personally held corporate stock, 77 percent of the value of trusts, and 62 percent of state and local bonds.[15]

---

retirement), whereas capital wealth is accumulated for other reasons (power and control). Capital wealth is closest to our material concept of capital, and the people (families) holding it constitute the class of the same name. E. N. Wolfe, "The Size Distribution of Household Disposable Wealth in the United States," *Review of Income and Wealth* 29 (June 1983), 125–46.

[15] From the July 1986 report, *The Concentration of Wealth in the United States*, written by the Joint Economic Committee of the U.S. Congress, and from subsequent revisions to its data. The Survey Research Center of the University of Michigan gathered data for the report and the Federal Reserve Board compiled them. Revised figures corrected a data entry error that had overstated unincorporated business asset holdings of the wealthy, but few of the revised figures were made public. The following tables summarize revised data and original data that were unaffected by the error:

Distribution of wealth in the United States (assets after deduction of debt)

Families	Shares of wealth owned, including homes 1983	1963
Top 0.5%	26.9%	25.4%
Top 10%	66.9%	65.1%
Remaining 90%	32.1%	34.9%

Sources: Joint Economic Committee of the U.S. Congress, *Concentration of Wealth in the United States*, July 1986, and *Wall Street Journal*, August 22, 1986.

Distribution of ownership of selected business assets, 1983

Families	Corporate stock	Bonds	Real estate (excluding private homes)
Top 0.5%	46.5%	43.6%	35.6%
Top 10%	89.3%	90.4%	77.8%
Remaining 90%	10.7%	9.7%	22.2%

Source: J.E.C., *Concentration of Wealth.*

Data from the July Joint Economic Committee study was widely reported in the press, partly because it showed a large increase in the share of wealth in the hands of the very wealthy. On the same day that it reported the revised figures, the *Wall Street Journal*, in its "Review and Outlook" section, claimed that the revised 1983 figures showed "no statistically significant increase in concentration of wealth" between 1963 and 1983. It offered no statistical evidence to support this claim, while the revised 1983 figures show a 5.9 percent increase in the amount of wealth held by the top half of one percent of families compared to 1963. *Either* of the 1963 or the 1983 figures illustrate our argument. U.S. Census Bureau data indicate growing disparity in *income* distribution over the past

The remaining 99.5 percent of households shares the rest, but none too equally. For instance, in 1983 the top 10 percent of households held two-thirds of the wealth, including homes for personal use. That means, of course, that the remaining 90 percent of American households held one-third of the wealth. We find little difficulty in applying the term "capital" to the people of these households—approximately 420,000 when addressing the top half of one percent in the U.S. distribution—who control such a disproportionate amount of wealth. Along with other common characteristics, people in these groups share a class concern for maintaining high profits and assuring private accumulation of capital. Class interests and the ways in which they impinge on community control of economic development must be made a part of our discussion.

In a capitalist world most decisions in the economy are carried out by a decentralized mix of private decision makers. Individual investors pool their funds in corporations, and corporations then commit those funds to producing goods and services in quest of profits or return on invested capital. Profits are lifeblood. Inability of the economy to generate them at a high enough rate is a sure indicator of an economy in trouble. If the profit rate drops, productive investment diminishes. People making investment decisions hold their funds in interest-bearing form (loans to others or to the government), or in speculative form (gold, for instance). Such temporary havens assure some return on capital along with relative security in uncertain times; they suffice until more assured opportunities for higher profits are created.[16] Since

---

decade. By 1986 the top 5 percent of families received more of aggregate income than did the bottom 40 percent of American families. See U.S. Bureau of the Census, *Statistical Abstract of the United States: 1988*, 108th ed. (Washington, D.C., 1987), p. 428, table 701. If income and taxation trends continue, it will not be many years before the top 1 percent of families in the United States will receive a larger portion of aggregate after-tax income than the lowest 40 percent of families.

[16] "Reaganomics" can be understood as a set of policies aimed at raising profitability in the capitalist system. By (a) implementing an anti-union drive in conjunction with a monetary policy–induced increase in unemployment which together held wages down, (b) boosting corporate after-tax profit potential through the 1981 tax revisions, (c) freeing business from "excessive" regulation, and (d) reemphasizing willingness to use force internationally to maintain U.S. spheres of influence for resource availability and access to global markets, the U.S. government was able to launch an extended but shaky boom for capital. It overcame some aspects of the stagnation of the previous decade, including some of the tendency for capital to be "on strike" until higher returns on new investment could be gained. Investors' willingness to carry out investment that would be productive of new surplus value was logically tied to their desire for increased potential for profit relative to the perceived risk of investment. New cycles of mergers and acquisitions also resulted,

they do not combine labor with capital, no surplus is produced through them. Interest is paid from surplus generated elsewhere in the economy; gains or losses incurred in speculation are ultimately paid from the same source.

In order for the rate of profit to be relatively high, costs of inputs used in producing goods and services must be kept down relative to final selling price. Inputs include raw materials that can escalate in cost (oil in the 1970s) and the human basis of all production, labor. Given enough consumer purchasing power in the economy to assure sale of goods and services brought to market, every business stands to gain more profit if it can keep its wage costs lower than those of competitors selling the same product, everything else being equal between them. Lower wages mean higher profits. The source of higher profit is greater surplus value created in the production process.[17] Profit is simply the name given to the portion of surplus that the capitalist manages to retain. Once profit is gained, the investor faces the choice of reinvesting it or using it for consumption. Investors, or the managers of their corporations or investment portfolios, make the decision. The economy is private not because people in it have private claim to personal property; that is nearly universal in the modern world. It is a private economy because means of production are privately owned, because the surplus produced from their use is privately appropriated, and because the decision to reinvest a gain in wealth or to consume it is private as well.

Even in this private economy, government has some ability to intercede and take action. It does so in the name of society as a whole.

---

activity that does not expand the potential for surplus production.

Contemporary theoretical arguments and empirical evidence on the central role of profits in capitalism are summarized in Anwar Shaikh, "The Falling Rate of Profit and Economic Crisis in the United States," in *The Imperiled Economy*, Book I, Robert Cherry et al., eds. (New York: Union for Radical Political Economics, 1987), 115–26. A contrasting view of profitability linked to social structures of accumulation is contained in David M. Gordon, Richard Edwards, and Michael Reich, *Segmented Work, Divided Workers* (New York, 1982). The French "regulation school" of radical analysis, exemplified by Michel Aglietta, *A Theory of Capitalist Regulation* (London, 1979), links an analysis of social and economic regulation with more structural economic theory. Harvey, *The Limits to Capital*, provides a summary of much of the literature on crisis up to approximately 1980.

[17] In the case of machinery and equipment, depreciation indicates useful capacity that has been spent over a given period and for which provision for replacement must be made. Depreciation is not part of social surplus, but it helps to define it since equipment is a necessary ingredient of the current level of production. Social surplus does not include the replacement cost of this equipment; it is surplus product.

It provides programs that aid development in general, such as building infrastructure for commerce. It aids particular groups in society, assisting capital owners in expanding investment overseas, aiding workers by assuring minimum levels of safety in the workplace, and assisting others through various social services. By manipulating fiscal and monetary policy it can leave households with more disposable income, stimulating consumer spending, or it can provide incentives for increased saving. It can tax corporations more heavily, cutting final return on investment, or it can stimulate new investment by reducing taxation of income used for reinvestment. More broadly, changes in many facets of government action—welfare spending, labor law, immigration policy, social security payout, excise taxes on consumption of luxuries, expansion or contraction of spending on the military—shape the conditions under which profit levels are determined and reinvestment decisions made. Government policy is a principal factor in shaping the ongoing contest between capital and labor over relative shares in what is produced and in shaping the terrain on which various factions of capital compete.[18]

Social Surplus: Invisible in Orthodox Economics

Despite our unorthodox perspective, conservatives and liberals would find much to agree with in this brief description of the contemporary actors and institutions involved in investment decisions. But the concept of social surplus is another matter. It is rarely used today and is repugnant to capitalism's staunchest defenders for reasons that deserve elaboration.

Orthodox economics, the mainstay of teaching and practice in the West, has developed as a body of knowledge used to explain the way the capitalist economy works. As a policy science it has instrumental ends: taming the dramatic swings apparent in the system's historical record and improving its present and future performance. Not sur-

[18] On the role of the state in capitalist society, and the effects of state policy on the viability of capitalism, see Martin Carnoy, *The State and Political Theory* (Princeton, N.J., 1984); Bob Jessup, *The Capitalist State: Marxist Theories and Methods* (New York, 1982); Fred L. Block, *Revising State Theory: Essays in Politics and Postindustrialism* (Philadelphia, 1987); Robert R. Alford and Roger Friedland, *Powers of Theory: Capitalism, the State, and Democracy* (New York, 1985); James O'Connor, *The Fiscal Crisis of the State* (New York, 1973); and Jurgen Habermas, *Legitimation Crisis*, trans. Thomas McCarthy (Boston, 1975).

prisingly for a policy science, it also carries a significant ideological burden.[19] This burden is reflected in theory that makes social surplus—clearly present in other economic systems, past and present—invisible as modern orthodoxy explains the working of the capitalist system. The heart of this accomplishment is found in distribution theory. How is the income from the capitalist system divided? From the early chapters of most introductions to the "dismal science," one learns of three factors of production: land, labor, and capital. Each factor receives return on income for the part it plays in production. Land gets rent, labor gets wages, and capital gets interest and profit. While more sophisticated texts may avoid such a simple presentation, they must eventually return to its basic logic. In microeconomics all of the revenue to a firm, net of costs for intermediate goods purchased from other firms, goes to these categories of "inputs." As mentioned earlier, macroeconomic national income accounting for gross national product uses precisely the categories of compensation of employees, net interest, rental income, and profits. Theoretical explanations of distribution developed by Alfred Marshall, J. B. Clarke, and other turn-of-the-century contributors to neoclassical economics continue to dominate orthodox thinking today.[20] In their competitive market model, factors of production are paid their marginal product, the monetary equivalent of their contribution to production. Normal profits are considered a cost of doing business; they are the payment to capital just high enough to maintain its commitment to the investment. Extra-normal profits are ephemeral bait for entrepreneurs; free entry allows others to infringe quickly on abnormally profitable situations, cutting prices in competitive markets until profit has returned to normal levels. The point is that when the process is complete, no surplus or residual exists whose distribution must still be decided. All factor owners receive their payment, and the impartial competitive markets

[19] An introduction to this issue can be found in Homa Katouzian, *Ideology and Method in Economics* (New York, 1980); see particularly chap. 6. An amusing discussion of the ideological origins of neoclassical economics is contained in Guy Routh, *The Origin of Economic Ideas* (Armonk, N.Y., 1975).

[20] For presentation and defense of this approach in a representative text in introductory economics, see William J. Baumol and Alan S. Blinder, *Economics: Principles and Policy*, 3d ed. (San Diego, Calif., 1985), chap. 33. Historical perspective on development of the theory can be found, in orthodox form, in Mark Blaug, *Economic Theory in Retrospect*, 3d ed. (New York, 1978). A radical understanding of that same history is presented in E. K. Hunt, *History of Economic Thought: A Critical Perspective* (Belmont, Calif. 1979).

determine their levels. Original factor endowments are not questioned, and neither, of course, is private ownership of them.

Contemporary and somewhat more realistic analysis recognizes power as an important, if secondary, determinant of relative income levels among factors. The impact of power on distribution is often assessed, and deviations from ideal market outcomes analyzed. Discrimination skews wage shares, and family ties often determine initial endowments of capital and perhaps proclivities for entrepreneurial activity. Liberal tinkering with public policy aims to ameliorate the worst effects of these outcomes. If the American dream is to be accepted, biases and problems must be seen as correctable within a generation or two by better policies and by individual effort and sacrifice.

Confronted with the most productive economic system yet known to humankind, we are left with the question of what happened to social surplus. It certainly exists, but it is hidden from view by a mix of economic theory and carefully structured ideology.

First, the ideology. In capitalism pure and simple, nothing belongs to society. The word "social" in "social surplus" draws quick response from defenders of the faith. Property, assets, and resources are either privately held or they belong to the government. In this view of the world, government holdings result from taxing away what belongs to individuals. The legitimacy of government holdings is called into question based on the sanctity of private property, on the rewards due factors of production (privately held), and on grounds of efficiency. Maximum efficiency in allocating resources is linked to the best possible chances for growth, and growth is seen as the outcome that will serve all of society. Popular thinking was especially affected in the 1980s by an ideological campaign that characterized government as an alien force in the realm of the economy. The idea that government could be the custodian of society's resources, much less its productive assets, is consistently under attack. Surplus produced in such an environment is by definition private. All that remains is a never-ending struggle over how much of each individual's income will be confiscated for the public maintenance of society.

Surplus—not social surplus—exists in this economic theory, even if the term is not used. People do receive the interest, rent, or profit earned by the factors they own. Others save from high salaries, and some even manage to save from wages. Unconsumed income of all kinds, pooled in firms and aggregated in financial institutions, is made available for new undertakings. New or expanded firms pursue profit, and in their quest provide society with goods and services. The modern large corporation may have assumed saving and investment functions once attributed to households and individual entrepreneurs, but it continues to accumulate surplus and put it to work. The immediate goal is profit, but the systemic outcome is privately appropriated surplus.

Social Surplus: The Radical Perspective

We have defined social surplus as that portion of the product of a society created in a given period of time, and neither consumed by those who produced it nor used for reproduction of the means of production. The term "surplus product" is generally applied to this fund when speaking historically across modes of production. Surplus product specific to the capitalist mode of production is known as surplus value. In radical analysis of this system, surplus value is the fund from which profits, rent, and income are drawn. A fundamental characteristic of all class societies, including capitalism, is that social surplus ends up in the hands of the dominant class.

Surplus is produced by those who work in society, those whose efforts contribute directly or indirectly, but in substantive terms, to the maintenance of life. Considerable debate continues over distinctions between productive, indirectly productive, and nonproductive labor,[21] but there is no question that many members of society are not expected to contribute to its product—those too old or too young or not healthy enough to work. Others could contribute, but are denied the ability to do so by the system's inability to provide full employment. Others physically capable of contributing to social product do not. They gain enough income to support themselves by simply owning assets employed in production or assets such as housing used in the maintenance of life. A society's rentiers are its most obvious parasites; with respect to production, ownership itself imparts no functional role.

[21] See, for instance, Michèle Barrett, *Women's Oppression Today* (London, 1980), chaps. 1 and 5. An overview of the debate is contained in E. K. Hunt, "Categories of Productive and Unproductive Labor in Marxist Economic Theory," *Science and Society* 18 (Fall 1979), 303–25. We will return to the issue of productive and unproductive labor in Chapter 2.

Investigation of the changing nature of twentieth-century capitalism—particularly radical analysis over the past two decades—emphasizes the growing proportion of the labor force engaged in nonproductive work. Workers who are increasingly needed to keep the system functioning, but who are unproductive, are employed in appropriation (accountants and attorneys); in advertising (concerned with realizing surplus through sale of commodities, rather than creating it); in control functions within production itself (supervisory staff necessary largely because of the alienated and alienating nature of work); and in designing and engineering product changes that serve no purpose but superficial product differentiation or planned obsolescence. Arguments of this kind emphasize the waste involved in the growing need for unproductive labor, waste in that the expenditures do not provide for goods or services that satisfy human needs.[22] These activities result from the inability of the capitalist economy to maintain itself on an even keel without them.

Profits claim a major portion of surplus product in the capitalist economy. They mark the most visible transfer of social surplus from those who produce it to those who appropriate it, legitimately under capitalist property rights. The profit dynamic in the system is obviously self-reinforcing; those who gain control over social surplus in the present are likely to hold claim to it in the future.

If payment to unproductive activity and claims through property ownership constitute major portions of the surplus product of any period, so too do state expenditures made possible by tax revenues. The dual role of the state in capitalist society (fostering private capital accumulation and legitimizing the process of private accumulation[23]) allows much state activity to be seen in final analysis as vital to maintenance and preservation of established patterns of appropriation and distribution. Little or no state activity directly produces surplus, although expenditures on industrial infrastructure and education, to name two categories, support its production. State expenditures of other kinds, even if essential to reproduction of the system, use surplus product. Maintenance of military forces and their perpetually newer

[22] See John Bellamy Foster's summary of the *Monthly Review* school's approach in his *Theory of Monopoly Capitalism* (New York, 1986), chap. 2. Another neo-Marxist and even more eclectic analysis of waste in the U.S. economy can be found in Samuel Bowles, David Gordon, and Thomas Weisskopf, *Beyond the Wasteland: A Democratic Alternative to Economic Decline* (New York, 1983).

[23] This summary is from O'Connor, *Fiscal Crisis of the State*, chaps. 1 and 3.

hardware is notable in this category, but military activity has also historically been a primary means of acquiring capital, labor, and resources to use in producing more surplus. And even if what it buys is unused, military spending by the state can be highly favorable to capital owners' profits. It acts as a form of redistribution within the society. Private appropriation of social surplus is central to this system and is at the heart of the conflict over the state's right to tax away portions of individual and corporate income. Historically, it also constitutes one part of what Marxists have seen as the most fundamental of contradictions within capitalism: the increasingly social nature of the production of surplus product, in tension with appropriation based on property rights unchangingly linked to the private ownership of means of production. Means of production result from past human labor, and they grow and develop quantitatively and qualitatively because of choices made by a society and because of sacrifices borne unevenly in it.

Even if private appropriation has historically speeded the development of productive capacities, private appropriation and control over surplus product hamper more qualitative aspects of development. For our investigation of communities and capital they do so by severely limiting people's capacity to govern themselves democratically and to plan together—to make conscious collective choices—for their future. According to the orthodox economic notions of private market allocation and distribution of resources, the very premises of such a concern are suspect. But when the historical significance of social surplus is recognized, when its use in investigating a different way of conducting the life of a society and its communities is explored, then private appropriation of surplus becomes a crucial issue indeed.

Improvement in a society's ability to produce social surplus offers the possibility of reducing the time members of society spend reproducing their needs. With diminished necessary labor time, people can gain greater freedom from necessary work, and more opportunity for developing nonwork-related human capacities. Private appropriation blocks human development. Only limited growth in freedom from necessity can be won; it comes about to the extent that real income increases faster than increases in what is deemed necessary to life and does so in diminishing work time. Both trends can be noted over time for portions of the population of a limited group of advanced industrial countries. But in much the same way that extreme global disparity exists in the process, so too does domestic uneven development. Many of the problems faced by regions, cities, towns, and neighborhoods in the United States, an admittedly particular advanced industrial country, can be understood as resulting from the private appropriation of social product.

The fundamental conflict of capitalist life is played out most acutely when capital and labor confront each other in the workplace. It is also played out increasingly at the level of the state. It has always existed at an intermediate level as well, between communities and capital, where ultimately the issue is control over social surplus.

2

Tracking Social Surplus

To be of practical use to community groups, planners, and analysts, social surplus has to be identifiable in economic activity. It is not a standard business accounting category, and the purpose of this chapter is to demonstrate ways in which it can be identified despite that obstacle. Here we will more frequently use the term "surplus value" to denote the specific form that social surplus takes in a system of capitalist production.

Both the magnitude and the distribution of surplus value produced from any economic activity are central issues in this analysis. First we will deal with the question of how much surplus is being produced. In conventional economic data, subtracting the wage bill (payments to labor employed in the production process) from value added (the value of a unit of production's or a geographical area's shipments minus cost of materials—machinery, equipment, raw materials, and intermediate goods) yields an approximation of surplus value. The wage bill no doubt includes wages and salaries of workers who are unproductive (e.g., supervisory personnel who serve a controlling rather than coordinating function),[1] but it can be used in this short route to estimating the magnitude of surplus value produced.

Another approach can be followed if conventional accounting data

[1] Much of the work of salaried staff in larger corporations is unproductive in that it does not create new value. It entails maintaining or changing title for products and selling goods or services so that the firm can realize their embodied value. See Foley, *Understanding Capital*, pp. 118–22, for basic definitions. The last part of this chapter deals with productive and unproductive activity at the level of the national economy.

are available for a particular firm by adding specific categories that are elements of surplus value. The most obvious among them include rent, interest payments, and before-tax profits, or after-tax profits and taxes paid. If accounting data for a specific firm are unavailable, then industry averages can provide a starting point that can be modified to suit the special characteristics of the case under study, yielding an approximation for the firm. Our microeconomic example in this chapter uses this approach.[2]

What happens to the surplus? This investigation is distributional and has two component parts. One is geographic and the other class-based. Geographically, is surplus that is generated in a locality used there?[3] Is it reinvested in the town, city, or region, and if not, where does it go? In class terms, what groups get the surplus? The simple answer is, of course, that it goes to capital. For a community, however, the class outcome is more complex, and it is tied to the geographic outcome. Does profit or rent go to local capitalists or landlords, and are they likely to reinvest it locally? If it ultimately accrues to stockholders of a large corporation as dividends or capital gains, how many of them are residents of the locality, and is their income likely to be spent or reinvested there? Is a portion of surplus paid out to high-salaried top management of the firm, and if so, do they spend or save money in the community or live, spend, and save elsewhere? Each of these questions, and many more generated by the particular economic circumstances of the area under study, must be resolved at some level of specificity. In many cases general data and reasonable assumptions can lead to a clear enough picture to draw appropriate conclusions.

Despite our focus on local economies, it is important to stress again that this is only one aspect of complex economic and human activity. Area economies are firmly embedded in regional, national, and global ones, and their local activity must be understood in its broader context. Local development is more complex than what can be described

[2] While there are problems associated with using value-theoretic categories intended for an aggregate economy to analyze microeconomic outcomes, we believe important insights can be gained in doing so. The principal problem is that disaggregation obscures the fact that wage rates, levels of profitability, and other important categories are socially and politically derived, rather than simply conditions of a local economy or firm. Wages and profits result from the historical playing out of basic contradictions in capitalist society as a whole—most notably, class struggle.

[3] Douglas Koritz provides important clarification of this issue in "Research Strategies in Regional Political Economics: Theory and Evidence from the Pittsburgh SMSA" (Ph.D. dissertation, University of Pittsburgh, 1988), chap. 3.

by changes in accepted economic indicators, but the studies reviewed here deal almost exclusively with them. The point is to be able to use this information as one part of a foundation for planning future community action.

Economic analysis pertinent to community, city, and regional areas exists in several forms. One presents basic accounting data for expenditures, investment, and inventories of principal actors in the economy. Another augments that information with a flow of funds analysis, often accompanied by estimates of the multiplier[4] effects of some types of economic activity. Another form makes use of technically sophisticated modeling of economic activity in an area; it is often used in order to estimate the impact of future changes to the economy. A fourth and more simple approach emphasizes the implications of a specific new addition to the economy. The brief presentation of examples of these techniques to follow is intended to highlight the information each provides and particularly emphasizes the contribution that an understanding of social surplus adds.

These examples begin with our own estimation of the likely contribution of a fast-food restaurant to local development. This project-specific form of analysis is relatively simple to do and often must be done quickly in response to new investment proposals facing the community. Firm-specific analysis can also provide essential information on the economy of a community dominated by a few businesses or institutions. Analyzing each of them can lead to a basic understanding of flows of surplus into, out of, and within the community. Next we review two studies at the mesoeconomic level,[5] one of a neighborhood's and the other an urban region's economy, for information they may contain about surplus value. Last, we turn to

[4] Multipliers are estimates of the ultimate impact of changes in important economic variables. In analyzing local economic activity, their principal use is to estimate the cumulative change in income that can be expected in the economy as a result of a change in spending by consumers, businesses, or government. That initial boost in spending gets respent many times, and its total impact can be several times the amount of the initial change. Bennett Harrison's investigation of multipliers in poor communities indicates that they can be quite low. See his *Urban Economic Development* (Washington, D.C., 1974).

[5] We use this term to represent a diverse world between microeconomics, representing the firm or consumer, and macroeconomics, representing the national or global level. Mesoeconomics (*mesos* from the Greek for intermediate) includes in our usage the range from local aggregates of the community up to the regional level of economic activity. Stuart Holland used the term "meso-economic power" to refer to large firms that increasingly dominate Western economies. See his *Capital versus the Regions* (New York, 1976), chaps. 5 and 8.

the macroeconomy and a summary of a recent study of surplus produced in the U.S. economy since World War II.

Evaluating New Investment

Fast food is big business; by 1987 Americans spent over $50 billion on quick meals away from home. The mom and pop diner or snack bar of thirty years ago has yielded quickly to the onslaught of uniform product, low price, quick service, and intensive advertising. Communities without nationally advertised fast-food restaurants often eagerly await the day when the golden arches sprout next door to the local car dealership. In many minds this symbolizes a coming of age, a legitimizing. They too can keep tabs on and contribute to the billions of hamburgers sold, joining the mainstream of America in its rush to consume burgers and fries.

But what really happens to a community with the arrival of the uni-burger? Our analysis shows that perhaps three-quarters of the money it spends at its burger emporium will leave the community. In addition, a significant amount of the money spent there will accrue to property owners as social surplus.

We provide here a close look at one of the major providers of fast food, McDonald's Corporation. Americans know this chain well; McDonald's alone captures about 20 percent of dollars spent on fast food in the United States. Slightly over half the U.S. population lives within a three-minute drive of a McDonald's outlet. The McDonald's system spends an estimated $1 billion per year on advertising to assure its products remain on our minds.[6]

Without access to financial reports for an individual unit, we turned to National Restaurant Association (NRA) figures for restaurants with a limited menu and no table service as the starting point for our analysis.[7] While not a direct match to any one chain, these averages provide a broad picture that can be modified when necessary to fit particular situations.

The average sales of a McDonald's unit were approximately $1.5

[6] John F. Love, *McDonald's: Behind the Arches* (New York, 1986), p. 3; McDonald's Corporation, *1988 Annual Report*, p. 26.

[7] National Restaurant Association, *Restaurant Industry Operations Report, 1987* (Philadelphia, 1987).

million in 1988.[8] Using NRA median percentages for income and expenses in relation to sales,[9] such a unit would generate expenses and profit as outlined in column one of Table 1.

We are interested in two critical issues. First, how much social surplus is generated in an operation of this kind? Second, where does it go? Working down the list of income and expenses, we begin with the total "cost of sales" (cost of goods sold) category of expense, which includes payments for items sold, raw materials, intermediate goods, and supplies that are made into finished products. Sales of these items to McDonald's units include profit and interest on trade credit to suppliers which constitutes surplus. If 10 percent of cost of sales is used as an estimate of the figure for surplus that remains with suppliers (below this figure capital would be apt to desert the industry for other investments), a year's operation of the average restaurant generates $52,050 in social surplus in this form (column two).

For some restaurants a significant portion of cost of sales—nearly 35 percent of total sales—would be spent in the region for meat, bread, condiments, and supplies, but that is not the case for many chain operations. McDonald's franchises and corporately operated units must buy most of their material inputs from approved suppliers. These suppliers are often willing captives of the McDonald's system; they exist to serve McDonald's and have grown with the company.[10] Fast-food restaurants, and particularly McDonald's, have turned to a limited number of suppliers to assure uniformity of product and quantity purchase discounts. Consolidation has curtailed local purchases of goods and local generation of surplus from these purchases. Perhaps the local rancher sells the steer that will end up in a fast-

[8] According to the McDonald's *1988 Annual Report*, restaurants open at least one year averaged $1.6 million in annual sales. Franchise and joint-venture operations have somewhat lower averages, so we have chosen the figure of $1.5 million as a reasonable approximation. Our inquiry was prompted in part by David Morris's brief comment that a Washington, D.C., McDonald's was "exporting" more than two-thirds of its gross revenue out of the area. See *The New City States* (Washington, D.C., 1982), p. 6. Checking the source of that information led us to very suggestive analyses, using conventional accounting categories, of the economy of the Adams Morgan section of Washington. These included William Batko, "The Business of Food" (unpublished, 1975), and William Batko, Patricia Connor, and James Taylor, "The Adams Morgan Business Sector: Paying for Other People's Development" (unpublished, 1975), both done for the Institute for Local Self-Reliance in Washington, D.C.

[9] NRA, *1987 Report*, pp. 100–101.

[10] Love, *McDonald's*, p. 326. For the story of the development of several suppliers with the growth of McDonald's, see chap. 14.

food hamburger, or the local paper mill makes the paper that is converted into paper napkins that find their way to the take-out window. Even if this is the case, both products reach the major fast-food chains through a centralized distribution system. Surplus is increasingly made in processing and distribution rather than production of basic raw materials, and it ends up in the hands of major holders of the stock of large corporations, not the local farmer or woodlot owner.

In estimating the profits, rent, and interest included in the price of goods sold to our McDonald's, we have purposely chosen conservative figures, estimates that will, if anything, understate our case. We then must estimate the portion of the 10 percent, or $52,050, that remains in the area. Given very limited purchases from local suppliers, most of the surplus—we estimate 80 percent—is lost to the community. As indicated in Column 3 of Table 1, export of surplus in this accounting category is estimated to be $41,640.

One of the appealing promises of a new fast-food restaurant is jobs. By convention the Restaurant Association labels as "controllable expenses" items ranging from payroll to repairs and maintenance. Wages to adult workers and payment to supervisory personnel up to assistant manager levels are below subsistence-level income. Teenagers who have all or most of their living expenses met by parents and adults in two-income families thus provide much of the labor pool for these positions. In some urban and suburban labor markets workers receive wages of $5 per hour or more, but given higher living costs, these wages still would not support single adults, much less families.

Management salaries are another matter. A franchisee who also manages a unit may draw a salary containing some part of surplus that would otherwise be extracted as profit. The determining element in the allocation will generally be the expected tax bite from each form of income. Company-owned units in fast-food chains pay somewhat higher wages and benefits than franchised units,[11] a reflection perhaps of small amounts of surplus used as incentives to employees (particularly managers and supervisors) to keep them operating profitably.

Payments for advertising and promotion are made from surplus.

[11] Alan B. Krueger, "Ownership, Agency and Wages: An Examination of the Fast-Food Industry," Working Paper No. 226, Industrial Relations Section, Princeton University, September 1987, p. 9.

Table 1. Social surplus: The case of a McDonald's restaurant unit

		(1)	(2)	(3)	
	Ratio of income and expenses to sales*	Dollars per year based on sales of $1.5 million per year	Social surplus	Local distribution of social surplus	
				in area	out of area
Total sales	100%	$1,500,000			
Total cost of sales	34.7	520,500	(10%) 52,050	(20%) 10,410	(80%) 41,640
Gross profit	65.3	979,500			
Other income	0.4	6,000			
Total income	65.5	982,500			
Controllable expenses					
Payroll	22.9	343,500			
Employee benefits	2.9	43,500			
Direct operating expenses	3.6	54,000			
Music & entertainment	0.1	1,500			
Advertising & promotion	3.1	46,500	(100%) 46,500	(50%) 23,250	(50%) 23,250
Utilities	3.5	52,500	(4%) 2,100	(25%) 525	(75%) 1,575
Administrative & general	5.0	75,000			
Repairs & maintenance	1.1	16,500			
Total controllable exp.	47.4	711,000			
Income before occupation costs	20.0	300,000			
Occupation costs					
Rent	6.8	102,000	(100%) 102,000	(10%) 10,200	(90%) 91,800
Property taxes	0.6	9,000	9,000	9,000	
Other taxes	0.3	4,500	4,500	(50%) 2,250	(50%) 2,250
Property insurance	1.1	16,500	(100%) 16,500	(10%) 1,650	(90%) 14,850
Total occupation costs	8.3	124,500			
Income before int. & deprec.	12.7	190,500			
Interest	1.7	25,500	(100%) 25,500	(25%) 6,375	(75%) 19,125
Depreciation	3.5	52,500			
Restaurant profit (on sales)	8.0	120,000	(100%) 120,000	(20%) 24,000	(80%) 96,000
Totals			$378,150	87,660	290,490
				$378,150	

*Median for limited menu, no table service, sandwiches/hamburger restaurants. National Restaurant Association, *Restaurant Industry Operations Report*, 1987, p. 100.
[a]Capitalist
[b]Petty bourgeoisie
[c]Professional managerial class
[d]Working class

They contribute nothing to the creation of the product or its delivery to the consumer. Some small part of most advertising has informational value, but it is still paid for out of surplus. McDonald's bills itself as the most advertised brand name in the world. Payments for advertising do go to local and regional advertising media, as McDonald's operators work through the advertising cooperatives of approximately 165 operators and with 65 advertising agencies to reach

(4)		(5)			
Social surplus: initial appropriation		Class distribution of privately appropriated surplus			
private	public	C.[a]	P.B.[b]	P.M.C.[c]	W.C.[d]
(100%) 52,050		(90%) 46,845	(10%) 5,205		
(100%) 46,500		(20%) 9,300	(30%) 13,950	(40%) 18,600	(10%) 4,650
(100%) 2,100		(100%) 2,100			
(100%) 102,000		(90%) 91,800	(10%) 10,200		
	(100%) 9,000				
	(100%) 4,500				
(100%) 16,500		(50%) 8,250	(20%) 3,300	(20%) 3,300	(10%) 1,650
(100%) 25,500		(90%) 22,950	(10%) 2,550		
(100%) 120,000		(50%) 60,000	(50%) 60,000		
364,650	13,500	241,245	95,205	21,900	6,300
$378,150		$364,650			

their markets.[12] We estimate that half of the advertising takes the form of payments to local agencies and media.

A large amount of energy is needed to keep a food-finishing factory in operation, and the typical fast-food restaurant spends as much on utilities as it does on advertising. Energy supply typically involves a payment to equity and debt holders of privately owned "public"

[12] Love, *McDonald's*, p. 227.

utilities and payment of high salaries to some utility managers. We make the assumption that 4 percent of payment for utilities goes to privately appropriated surplus, and that 75 percent of that amount leaves the local area.

The accounting category of occupation costs is at the heart of our concern for social surplus. The first item in this section is rent, the primary element of income to McDonald's Corporation. By 1982, McDonald's had surpassed Sears, Roebuck and Company as the world's largest owner of real estate. McDonald's owns the land and buildings of nearly two-thirds of its domestic stores, and its rental income constitutes 90 percent of the income the corporation receives from franchise units.[13] This income makes up approximately two-thirds of corporate income; the remaining third derives from the profit of units that McDonald's operates directly. For those, of course, its "rental payment" is to itself.

"Corporate entrepreneurs" often own multiple franchises. Unlike many fast-food operations, McDonald's does not give franchise rights to a territory; franchise owners get additional units only after proving their ability to operate existing units to the corporation's satisfaction. Franchises have generally been given for twenty years, to be renewed at the corporation's discretion.

Rent is paid by franchisees based on a basic minimum rental fee and a percentage of sales. McDonald's franchisees pay 8.5 percent of sales for use of the land, building, and basic equipment. This rental fee is distinct from the 3 percent of sales paid to the corporation as a service fee. NRA data understate the typical McDonald's rental payment, but we will use it to be consistent in estimating surplus conservatively. Of the 9,300 McDonald's units in operation in 1985, only 500 were paying the minimum rental fee.[14] The remaining 8,800 stores paid the highest average percentage of sales for rent in the fast-food industry. It accrues to McDonald's Corporation to be shared eventually as profit and capital gains to stockholders. To the extent that some stockholders live in the community where a sales unit is located, a portion of rent might be returned and respent in the community.

How did McDonald's get in a position to receive this rent? Doing

[13] Ibid., pp. 283, 159.
[14] Ibid., p. 158.

so took entrepreneurial acumen, work to develop its products, and the cash flow to advertise and to acquire assets. By the late 1950s, McDonald's cash flow enabled it to begin acquiring land, constructing its own buildings, and equipping them. Where did funds for acquisition of land come from? Franchisees who do not own their land and building rent from the company. They have been required to put up security deposits, half of which are refunded to them in ten years and the other half at the end of their franchise agreement in twenty years. The security deposit frequently was the corporation's down payment on the land it acquired, and future payments were made from rent charged to the franchise.[15] The separate franchise purchase fee provided McDonald's with the funds to leverage a mortgage for the building and equipment package. McDonald's financial strength grew with the suburban commercial real estate boom and the inflation that pushed up the value of their property. The corporation now owns approximately 60 percent of its real estate locations worldwide, and 68 percent of its domestic locations.[16]

McDonald's controlled costs by acquiring land and building early in its development period with mortgages from local banks. Some payments for land and building and the interest on locally borrowed funds constituted social surplus that may have been retained locally. But by the early 1960s McDonald's was negotiating major debt financing through insurance companies and large commercial banks and diminishing the time spent in negotiating local financing for each unit of its expansion. Since a small minority of units have fixed payment leases, some rent does flow to landowners or building owners who live near their units; we have estimated that 10 percent of rental fees may return to the area.

Property taxes are a form of surplus flowing to the local community, city, and county. They help pay for the schools that educate McDonald's workers and for the roads that bring customers to them. Property taxes and the category "other taxes" (from Table 1) are resources generated by the unit which are shifted to public control

[15] Ibid., pp. 164–70. Later it began to buy back franchises, including one group of forty-three stores in the Washington, D.C., area owned by two Virginia businessmen. They had purchased each franchise and located them on their own land, so they paid McDonald's only the 3 percent service fee. The units eventually became part of the corporate group and pumped surplus to McDonald's rather than franchise owners.

[16] McDonald's, *1988 Annual Report*, p. 20.

and use. Units also collect sales tax for state and local governments, a percentage of sales that is of course paid directly by customers. It is not accounted for in a unit's financial statements.

Insurance is paid from social surplus. Conceptually it is similar to advertising, since it does not contribute to the goods or services produced. It may be underwritten by local agents or sales offices, but it accrues primarily to major insurance companies. Surplus paid out in this form is apportioned so that 10 percent of it ends up with a local agency and the rest with the insurer.

Since our discussion of fast-food restaurant chains has used McDonald's as an example, one additional feature of this company should be noted. McDonald's has been a leader in developing systematic local contributions to charities. This has been an effective means of countering negative aspects of the company's image, especially at the community level. Local operators direct contributions to high profile, all-American recipients such as schools, local youth bands, hospitals, and the Girl Scouts and Boy Scouts. Ronald McDonald Houses, providing assistance to families of seriously ill children, are developed and supported by local operators, not the company. By 1988 there were 118 of these houses in six countries. As McDonald's own publication puts it, "We share our success with our neighbors because they contribute to that success,"[17] a reminder to its operators of the source of their wealth. In the mid-1980s, one observer of the McDonald's system estimated that it gave 4 percent of corporate and franchise pretax profit to local causes.[18] The fact that charitable contributions do not appear as a distinct entry in the National Restaurant Association accounting averages is evidence of the unusual nature of this level of giving in the restaurant industry.

Three major categories remain. The first is interest: rent paid for the use of liquid assets. A McDonald's franchisee typically will borrow part of the franchise fee to buy the license and kitchen equipment, furnishings, and sign package from the corporation (at a cost of $400,000 in 1986[19]); the corporation would finance about half that fee. Some restaurants may also pay interest to suppliers for trade credit or to local banks for borrowed working capital. Franchisees who have purchased their own land or building will also pay interest

[17] Ibid., p. 24.
[18] Love, *McDonald's*, p. 213.
[19] Ibid., p. 371.

on funds borrowed for the purpose. In the typical McDonald's arrangement, little interest will flow from franchisee to the local economy. Some may flow from the McDonald's Corporation to a former local landowner who has sold commercial real estate to McDonald's. Given McDonald's major institutional financial ties, we can reasonably assume that most interest payments are from the franchisee to the franchiser or its supporting financial institutions. Even fast-food restaurants with more "local" financing may still be paying interest to a branch of a major U.S. or international bank, in which case it is quickly pooled for lending anywhere. We have conservatively estimated that three-quarters of interest payments leave the community.

Depreciation is a noncash expense that cannot be counted as part of social surplus. Surplus is net of costs of replacing existing productive resources. Although the amount of depreciation reported by businesses is clearly determined by existing tax regulations and the taxpayer's desire to minimize reported taxable income, we assume that reported depreciation bears some relationship to replacement costs for expended assets and leave it out of our calculation of surplus.

Profit concludes the accounting tableau; it is generally singled out as the one category of income that a business operator takes out of a community. Local taxes typically are not paid on profit. State or federal taxes may be. This "reward to entrepreneurship" is pure social surplus. NRA data for 1987 point to a profit rate for fast-food restaurants of 8 percent of sales. The industry average has dipped since that time, because intense competition in some areas has resulted from overbuilding relative to growth in consumer demand. McDonald's units, on the other hand, have shown profits in the range of 15 percent of sales in recent years.[20] We use the 8 percent figure to keep our estimate of surplus on the conservative side and to make it more representative of fast-food restaurants in general. Profit goes to the franchise owner—or to McDonald's stockholders if the unit is part of the McDonald's Operating Company. The franchise owner may or may not live in the area or reinvest his or her money there.

Column 2 of Table 1 summarizes the estimates of social surplus made for our hypothetical fast-food restaurant. Surplus is far higher than profit as traditionally defined for such a business; based on our

[20] Eric N. Bern, "How Two Burger Flippers Stack Up," *New York Times*, Nov. 30, 1988. Average annual profits of a McDonald's unit with sales of $1.5 million have been reported to be $234,000, or 15.6 percent of sales.

conservative estimates, it is over three times the amount of profits alone for this type of operation. The surplus was drawn from the income of people who patronize the restaurant and was created by those who work in it. Twenty-five percent of the money spent by patrons at this restaurant emerges as social surplus.

Geographical distribution of surplus is clearly tied to class distribution, but Table 1 separates them to bring both into focus. By definition, franchise owners of these restaurants are not poor people, and they are unlikely to be residents of poor areas. Surplus from an operation in a poor, inner-city neighborhood will go to an owner living (and spending) in a higher-income part of the city or in a suburb. Profits that flow to corporate headquarters ultimately end up in the accounts of stockholders. With the wealthiest 10 percent of U.S. families owning close to 90 percent of stock held by individuals (see chapter 1, note 15), profits are distributed to a select group of communities. Surplus that accrues to pension funds reaches a somewhat broader but still restricted segment of the U.S. population. International stockholding draws a portion of profit to the accounts of the wealthy in other parts of the world. Based on our estimates of geographical distribution of surplus (column 3), 77 percent of surplus leaves the area.

Surplus extracted from a community returns to it only if it is attracted by the favorable investment environment, if it is in the form of transfer payments from tax revenue or charitable gifts, or through goods or services purchased there. In lieu of these transactions, development is short-circuited. A new restaurant, perhaps welcomed by a community desperate for jobs and development, can turn out to be a suction pump extracting the essential material basis for further development. Subsistence-level jobs and the training for work that goes with them can be a boon to poor communities, but little else is realized.

Other forms of business also extract a major share of money paid to them by community residents. The auto dealership located next to McDonald's provides an example, as the car dealer must buy the car to be sold and payment for it flows to an auto producer. Economics of scale in production provide some grounds for the size of the auto producer, but the same is not the case for a restaurant. Shared economies in advertising and mass purchasing of inputs, and a deskilled production process, are more vital to the chain restaurant operation. Beef, bread, and potatoes are often produced locally, but the chain's corporate-linked purchasing eliminates local suppliers. In terms of job creation, auto mechanics and salespeople require skills and knowledge, and can claim income, that the fast-food worker cannot.

Column 4 of Table 1 summarizes our estimate of the division of surplus between private and public appropriation as it is reflected through accounting data of this kind. Ninety-six percent of the surplus generated is privately appropriated. Property taxes and other local taxes amount to a meager 4 percent of total surplus. The accounting data indicate profit before income tax is paid by the franchisee. The traditional means of appropriating more surplus for public use has been through income tax. The franchise may be able to reduce further taxable income by means of expenses of the business entity holding the franchise, but some federal income tax will be paid by a profitable franchise. Income distribution to owners will be taxed at current rates of 28 or 33 percent. The state in which the franchisee lives may also require an income tax payment. Operating profit that flows to McDonald's Corporation, as well as its rent and interest income, is subject to corporate income tax after it is reduced by the corporation's expenses. McDonald's estimated its current and deferred income tax for 1988 at $400,600,000, including federal, state, and international payments. The figure was 38 percent of the corporation's reported taxable income of slightly over a billion dollars.[21]

Column 5 is a speculative estimate of the class character of the privately distributed social surplus (located in column 4). It uses four class formations to estimate the major recipients of this income. Revenues from payments to advertising and insurance firms are spread across all groups in our approximation of who would benefit from them. The two primary classes with respect to this distribution are capital, with nearly two-thirds of it, and the petty bourgeoisie. In typical class analyses of advanced capitalism, members of the petty bourgeoisie are small business operators caught in precarious conditions between significant property ownership (the capitalist class) and a return to dependence on wage or salary income (the working class or professional managerial class). Owners of one or two McDonald's franchises and little else could be counted in the upper reaches of the petty bourgeoisie.

Summarizing the analysis, resources generated from this hypothetical new business stand a limited chance of being used for further

[21] McDonald's, *1988 Annual Report*, pp. 27–32.

local development. Most of the surplus is privately appropriated, the majority of it leaves the area, and its class distribution highly favors those who already have access to substantial wealth.

Fast-food franchise restaurants are part of contemporary American life, and they are rapidly becoming the norm in other parts of the world as well. Principled opposition to them can be made on grounds of environmental degradation (destruction of tropical areas for raising beef cattle; mountains of nonbiodegradable trash for landfills), proliferation of dead-end jobs (low skill, minimum wage, part-time work with little room for advancement), and the nature of the products they serve (food products with high fat and high salt content). We have highlighted a different aspect of their presence in the community. Compared to the locally owned and operated, independent restaurant or diner, fast-food franchises reflect and contribute to concentration and centralization of capital. Chains such as McDonald's and Burger King grow as they reinvest profits, and as their sizes increase they can enter more and more local economies, nationally and internationally. The usual meaning of the term centralization of capital is that some firms grow larger through their accumulation of surplus value. Centralization takes place in terms of large firms taking over segments of the restaurant food market and eliminating independent producers. Fast-food franchises simply drive local competitors out of business.

Facing this onslaught, most communities opposed to it have acted on two options. One has been to recognize the nature of the beast and its probable impact on any new home it chooses and to ban it by indirect means such as zoning regulation. For instance, the town of Saugatuck, Michigan, held off an initial attempt by McDonald's to locate in its commercial zone because of a shortage of parking in the area.[22] Given the legal resources of these firms and popular demand for their heavily advertised products, this is more than likely a short-term response. Another option has been to allow establishment of restaurants of this kind but to regulate them closely. What they look like, whether or not they are allowed to include drive-through service, and the minimum wage they will pay are subject to local, regional, and national regulation.[23]

[22] Isabel Wilkerson, "Midwest Village, Slow-Paced, Fights Plan for Fast-Food Outlet," *New York Times*, July 19, 1984.

[23] Most fast-food restaurants, and McDonald's particularly, have shown a willingness to modify building and sign designs in response to opposition to their locating in communities. For instance, residents in Old Anacostia in Washington, D.C., worked with McDonald's

Recognizing the economic impacts reflected in the example presented above, some communities have chosen a third response: invest in a franchise. They get everything that a private investor does—a proven operating system, technical assistance, accepted products, and profit. The profit stays in the community where it is used to fund other community-based activity. We will investigate this new form of community enterprise in Chapter four.

From Neighborhood to Region: The Mesoeconomy

Community-based economic analysis is difficult and time-consuming work. Information is scattered among numerous public agencies and private organizations or must be gathered from original sources. Information already in the hands of organizations may or may not be available to a community group, and what is available may be dated, poorly gathered, or for various reasons incompatible with other essential data. The fact that the work is time consuming means that it is expensive to do.

We have been surprised by what appears to be a lack of current work on local economic analysis; it somehow has fallen out of fashion, at least as practical activity. Academic research continues to expand techniques and computer applications in the field, but few local governments pursue its more routine forms. Practitioners, planners, and local officials offered several responses to our question of why practical work of this kind seems less common now than a decade ago. Their reasons include greatly reduced federal funding for local economic studies; reliance on well-known and universally applicable local development strategies (e.g., import substitution and export expansion); and the difficulty for local officials and funding agencies to justify the time and costs of doing these studies, combined with the uncertainty or imprecision of their results. Even if they are done by knowledgeable and thorough analysts, other experts can be found to challenge their assumptions, argue that different data should have been used, estimate different multipliers, or question survey tech-

---

to see that its design fit the historical characteristics of its site. The city of Ithaca, New York, extracted similar concessions for a McDonald's located in an old building on its downtown pedestrian mall. Battles over use of drive-through windows, which can have significant impact on sales volume and profitability, have been more contentious. Drive-through windows are typically controlled by zoning or environmental regulations.

niques. Each of these assertions contains elements of truth, but even taken together they do not comprise a conclusive argument against gathering, organizing, and analyzing information on local economic activity.

Review of these studies suggests that groups planning to do them must begin with a clear idea of their objectives and pay careful attention to the amount of information necessary to meet their needs. Given our objectives, we were especially interested in studies that provide information on flows of funds into and out of areas, circulation of funds in the study area, and distributional aspects of the flows.

East Oakland's Economy

Our review of useful studies of community, city, or regional economies begins with a comprehensive 1979 survey of East Oakland, California, by Community Economics. East Oakland stretches from a port area on San Francisco Bay eastward through industrial areas, mixed commercial, residential, and industrial areas; residential neighborhoods; and commercial strips. The city provides housing for half of Oakland's residents and it includes a high proportion of poor residents and a large minority population. It is also characterized by population decline and aging housing stock. Pockets of East Oakland were beginning gentrification in the late 1970s, when demand for moderate cost housing in the Bay Area was pushing housing costs up rapidly. Declining job opportunities in manufacturing was an attribute that East Oakland shared with many American cities. Growth was expected in white-collar and clerical jobs; in the financial sector, government, and service work, and in construction in Oakland's redeveloping downtown district. At the time of the study the unemployment rate of East Oakland residents was approximately three times that of the San Francisco-Oakland SMSA (Standard Metropolitan Statistical Area). With changing shopping patterns and a relatively poor population, East Oakland's retail shops and service outlets had been in steady decline.[24]

Community Economics's evaluation of income and consumer spending patterns in East Oakland began by documenting the fact

[24] Laura J. Henze, Edward Kirshner, and Linda Lillow, *An Income and Capital Flow Study of East Oakland, California*, prepared for the Charles Stewart Mott Foundation by Community Economics (Oakland, Calif., 1979), pp. 6, 22, and 7–11. This study is available from Community Economics, 1904 Franklin Street, Suite 900, Oakland, CA 94612.

that residents had incomes well below Bay Area and national levels. Within the community, low income, "flatland" areas had 30 percent less wage and salary income than "hill area" residents, and approximately one-quarter of their interest, dividend, and "other" income.[25] In sum, the poorest of East Oakland's residents had little income, savings, or property.

The study estimated household consumer spending patterns from available data and compared them to national averages. Predictably, housing, food, and transportation were the top three categories in each group of data; however, the figure that stands out in comparison with national data was the cost of housing. The shelter component (mortgage or rent payment, insurance, maintenance, repairs) accounted for 22 percent of residents' spending, compared to a national average of 16 percent. Other levels of spending were within a percentage point of national averages, except for fuel and utilities, which was only 3 percent of total spending, compared to 5 percent nationally. The tax bill of East Oakland's residents was more than offset by their income in the form of transfer payments.[26]

Housing took center stage in this study. The community contained a high percentage of renters compared to owners of housing and a high percentage of absentee landlords. Approximately two-thirds of rental housing of two to four units had landlords who were East Oakland residents, but two-thirds of landlords of single family homes and rentals of five or more units lived outside the community. Community Economics estimated that in 1978, $43 million of $77 million in rent payments went to landlords who did not live in East Oakland. Much of that money was lost to the community. Mortgage payments totaled an estimated $56 million, of which $40–45 million were interest payments.[27] In addition, fees estimated at 8.5 percent of the purchase price of housing that was sold in any period were paid as

[25] Ibid., p. 16 and table III-2, p. 19.

[26] Income figures for the study were derived from U.S. Census data, Community Economics's estimates based on its own survey, and Internal Revenue Service and Bureau of Economic Analysis data. Spending patterns were estimated from U.S. Department of Labor, Bureau of Labor Statistics, *Consumer Expenditure Surveys*. Appendix I of the study provides general information on income and capital flow studies and the significance of the expenditure multiplier for communities. Other appendixes provide useful information on conducting such a study, a sample of the resident survey instrument used, and a guide to data sources. Henze, Kirshner, and Lillow, *Income and Capital Flow Study*, table III-6, p. 27, and p. 26.

[27] Ibid., pp. 39, 32.

"closing costs" by local residents, much of it to outside banks and attorneys.

Recommendations addressing clear problems in the housing sector were divided into short- and long-term strategies. They were designed to retain community housing dollars and recycle them more fully and to protect residents who were being adversely affected by fast-rising housing costs. Short-term measures included limitations on rent increases, limits on condominium conversion of rental housing, and a city tax on short-term capital gains on sales of rental properties. Recommended longer-term efforts were conversion of rental housing to cooperative ownership and expanded housing stock rehabilitation programs.[28]

Data on housing indicated a need to examine closely flows of credit and capital. Comparing data on new nonresidential construction, residential construction, and business investment in East Oakland with Oakland and surrounding communities, analysts demonstrated East Oakland's relatively weak performance in attracting its share of investment. Neighborhood commercial areas were among the hardest hit in terms of lack of new investment, reflecting the trend to more mall shopping, and in terms of investment in Oakland's downtown redevelopment.[29]

Credit for housing transactions was available, but not from conventional home lenders. Although residents placed their savings in commercial banks and savings and loan associations, nearly half of the mortgages for East Oakland residents were provided by mortgage companies. In the rest of Oakland, mortgage companies accounted for less than one-eighth of housing loans. In some cases mortgage companies acted as agents for government-guaranteed loans, but in instances where they provided direct mortgages, they did so at interest rates 3 to 6 percentage points above those charged for conventional lender mortgages. The study estimated the cost of this added interest burden on the community to be substantial and ongoing. The same pattern was found in consumer and small business credit available to residents. The study did not provide information on the percentage of local ownership in banks and mortgage companies, but it is reasonable to assume that even if they had Bay Area owners, they were unlikely to spend much of their profits in East Oakland. At the time

[28] Ibid., pp. 44–51.
[29] Ibid., pp. 65–67.

of the study, East Oakland did have one locally organized credit union. Not surprisingly, expanding access to forms of credit at rates similar to those in other parts of the city was given high priority in the report's recommendations. The report also recommended use of the Community Reinvestment Act, which was enacted in the year prior to the study to expand access to credit in existing financial institutions, and establishment of more community-based financial institutions.[30]

In addition to the availability of housing and credit, another major area of concern to those conducting the study was East Oakland's commercial sector. Approximately $150 million of the $450 million that residents spent on consumer goods in 1978 was spent outside the community. An estimated two-thirds ($85 million of $125 million) in wages, rents, and profits paid out by stores based in East Oakland left the community as well. One nearby major shopping mall included less than 5 percent of East Oakland's retail outlets, but captured 13 percent of its consumer dollars. Sixty-five percent of locally based businesses and 75 percent of other businesses had owners who lived elsewhere.[31]

The study recommended a community-based strategy for revitalizing East Oakland's commercial sector and estimated gains that could be won through additional recirculation of local dollars. Increasing credit availability and technical assistance for locally owned small businesses, clustering commercial properties and making them more accessible, and expanding the activities of community development corporations in services offered to minority entrepreneurs in job skills training and in local ownership of buildings were suggested.[32]

Information derived from this study provided a picture of a community whose economy had been hemorrhaging for some time. Its results directed attention to vital areas of difficulty, enabling community groups to target them more constructively. Uncovering patterns of ownership of commercial and housing assets and the flows of funds resulting from ownership patterns helped explain the community's plight. The study was made available to community groups and served as a resource for initiatives to reverse the decline of East Oakland.

[30] Ibid., pp. 68, 76–79.
[31] Ibid., pp. 54, 55, and 56.
[32] Ibid., pp. 61–63.

Chester and Regeneration

Chester, Pennsylvania, shares many of East Oakland's problems. Located on the Delaware River just south of Philadelphia, it has a population of approximately forty five thousand people. Chester was Pennsylvania's first city, but it is now described as a geographic entity, not an economic one.[33]

On a map Chester appears to be a suburb of Philadelphia, and in some ways it is. But this is not the prestigious Main Line: New malls and major retailers are not opening here, and the physical environment is not one of manicured lawns and handsome shade trees. Chester provides a portion of Philadelphia's workers, yet 42 percent of its workforce is employed in Chester itself—in manufacturing, construction, industrial services and waste processing, and small retail establishments. Only five percent of businesses employ over one hundred people. The population is 57 percent African-American.[34]

Suspecting (and hoping) that Chester was ripe for development, community leaders formed the Chester Regeneration Project to stimulate, to control, and to assess the potential for future development. They turned to the Regeneration Institute, affiliated with the Presbyterian Church and Rodale Press's technical assistance group (now the Rodale Regeneration Project), to complete a study of their local economy and to chart locally based development strategies. That work was completed in 1987.[35]

The regenerative community development strategy is straightforward: build on local strengths to decrease the vulnerability of a local economy to outside forces and "create the greatest long-term benefit

[33] *The Local Economy Inventory Report for Chester, Pennsylvania,* 4 Vols., prepared for the Chester Regeneration Project by RPM Systems, Inc. (New Haven, Conn., 1987), 1:12 and 31.

[34] Ibid., pp. 27, 13.

[35] *The Local Economy Inventory Report* is a combination of business surveys of the local economy, a compilation of demographic, economic, and financial data from standard sources. A mailing list of 525 Chester businesses was compiled from the most recent *Pennsylvania Industrial Directory*, *Dalton's Delaware County Directory*, and the *Electronic Yellow Pages*. Each company received a detailed survey with cover letters from the Chester Regeneration Project president and Chester's mayor, asking for information on sales and markets, personnel and staffing, waste generation, technical assistance utilization, and bank use. Thirty-seven firms responded, and four additional survey forms were returned after initial data analysis. The low response rate sent the research team back to secondary sources such as Dun & Bradstreet's electronic database and the *Electronic Yellow Pages* in order to flesh out basic information on the remaining firms. Census material from 1980 and municipal government sources were also used.

to the greatest number of people in the community by utilizing the community's resources and economic strengths most effectively."[36] The method this strategy uses for development consists of import substitution and retention of community members' income for more extensive circulation in the community.

Unemployment in Chester in 1980 was 12.5 percent. Census measurement of population showed an 18.7 percent decline since 1970. Household income in 1980 was less than $10,000 for almost half the residents.[37] These and other commonly accepted indicators of community well-being characterized Chester as a city in need of regeneration. From estimates of personal spending found in *The Local Economy Inventory Report for Chester, Pennsylvania*, researchers drew attention to high percentages of expenditures for energy, food, and housing. They then estimated how large a portion of expenditures for these three items flowed out of the community. The conclusion was that most of the dollars spent for large and essential items left the community, flowing to and benefiting institutions and individuals located elsewhere.

The high energy expenditures of Chester's residents distinguish their city from East Oakland. The expenditures were attributed not only to a colder climate but also to high energy costs and a high proportion of energy-wasteful housing. While some of the estimated $60 million per year spent on energy went to local retailers and distributors, gas and electric utilities were located elsewhere. Given the income profile of the community, surely very little of the profit or interest paid by those utilities to owners and lenders returned to Chester. The study estimated that over 70 percent of food expenditures flowed directly out of Chester. Fifty-four percent of homes were owner-occupied, but since there were no community-based banks, mortgage payments flowed out of the community, primarily through branches of Philadelphia banks. No data were presented to indicate local or absentee levels of ownership of rental housing stock, and thus it is unclear how much of rental payments left the community.[38]

[36] Ibid., 1:3.

[37] Ibid., pp. 12–13.

[38] Ibid., pp. 17, 29. The report does not distinguish between mortgage and rental payments for housing. Its statement that "virtually all of the $70 million of rent and mortgage payments flow out of Chester" (1:17) appears to be based on the location of banks serving Chester, not on specific information included in the report on the ownership pattern of Chester's rental property.

The basis for this study's critical diagnosis of Chester's ailing economy resulted from input-output analysis. It demonstrated that only sixteen cents of every dollar of income flowing to households, businesses, and government agencies were being generated locally. Expenditures by these institutions for goods and services were even less locally based, with thirteen cents of each dollar spent with local providers.[39] In sum, small amounts of the income and expenditures that flowed into and out of Chester went through local circulation, resulting in little generation of businesses and jobs in the community.

The Chester Regeneration Project based its strategy on these findings. Researchers recommended creation of "pathways for money to flow within the community as well as out of it."[40] They included seeking matches between local needs and local providers, and gaining markets for local firms by meeting the needs of Philadelphia area businesses. Coordination, planning, technical assistance, and fund-raising to set these developments in motion would be coordinated through the Chester Regeneration Project. Developments of this kind require local cohesion and leadership. From our understanding of the project's history, maintaining a strong enough local base of support for the regeneration strategy has proven difficult.[41] Whether Chester will be able to sort out its own path to development or be further buffeted—for better or worse—by outside forces of change remains unclear.

The East Oakland and Chester studies share what might be described as "appropriate technologies" for analyzing local economic activity. Studies of this kind can be done by local organizations or government staff members. Of the two studies, the East Oakland one is more rigorous, its results are available to the public, and its authors were careful to include extensive information on sources and data-handling techniques.

The following two studies are more sophisticated in technique, and they attempt to develop more complex information for larger geographical areas. While their execution would call for skills and computer resources that local organizations and governments may not

[39] Ibid., pp. 32–35. Material presented in the study is based on 1979 data that are converted to 1986 levels by use of a CPI multiplier. The composite totals are derived from estimated percentages in each category of income and expenditures.

[40] Ibid., p. 32.

[41] Based on telephone interview with William Cohea, director of the Regeneration Institute, April 28, 1989.

possess, variations on either study could be accomplished for local interests by hired expertise or perhaps by area universities.

The Cleveland Area Study

Input-output analysis is used extensively in the study of national and regional economies. One extension of this technique in particular holds promise for enhancing the study of local economies and for determining the impact of new projects or investment on them. We will discuss it after reviewing the technique and a more traditional example of its application.

The basic input-output approach owes its modern form to the Nobel laureate Wassily Leontief.[42] Leontief's development of input-output marked a major step toward empirical analysis of production for a modern economy. It is a technical investigation of what output can be produced, including the amounts of intermediate goods that will be used up in production given a particular level of technology and available quantities of resources. It is considered a general equilibrium approach in economics because it takes account of the interdependence of various production sectors of the economy; each uses the products of others in making its own products.

Input-output analysis serves several significant purposes. It provides a detailed structure for national income accounting, it can serve as a planning tool if demand estimates are obtained, and it can identify what portion of total productive activity can be used for consumption, as compared to production. The analysis itself uses a matrix format and the solution of a set of simultaneous linear equations of the same number as the set of designated variables. Debate continues on how best to account for technical problems as this form of analysis is refined and as its applications expand.[43] Our concern lies with some of its applications.

Regional and local economies challenge us to understand them as active parts of larger economic systems. Aaron Gurwitz and Thomas Kingsley present a representative application of input-output analysis

[42] For a collection of articles reflecting the development and some applications of this technique, see Wassily Leontief, *Input-Output Economics*, 2d ed. (New York, 1986).

[43] Among the problems of input-output analysis are two unrealistic assumptions: (1) that no two commodities are produced by the same industry (this can be modified in practice, where joint production can be accommodated in calculations) and (2) that input proportions in production are fixed, so that inputs increase in use proportionally as production increases.

to a local economy in *The Cleveland Metropolitan Economy*.[44] Commissioned by the Cleveland Foundation, a group of public- and private-sector leaders in the Cleveland area, the study was intended as a means of establishing a database on local economic conditions and as a foundation for future information-gathering and analysis. The study covered the four-county Cleveland SMSA consisting of the City of Cleveland and its suburbs. Input-output analysis, used in traditional fashion, enabled development of a general picture of employment in Cleveland's industries and services, an estimate of the percentage of employment attributable to exports by industry, and estimates of growth rates by industry. Conventional earnings multipliers, which estimate how great a gain in local income will result from an increase in export business for a particular activity (presented as a multiple of a dollar of new export sales), were also developed for each industry or service. Multipliers were estimated for thirty two activities in durable goods and nondurable manufacturing sectors, sales, services, and an "other" category (transportation, communications). The multipliers ranged from a low of 1.50 (leasing) to highs of 2.88 (other transport equipment manufacturing) and 2.89 (insurance).[45] Although the authors made no claim for the high precision of these figures, their representation of gross differences across sectors was deemed a reasonable estimate of contributions made to the local economy by export activities.

The study of Cleveland painted an impressively detailed picture of the economy. It helped establish clearer understanding of patterns of employment gain and loss across sectors of the economy and between the city and suburban areas. Even though much employment growth had taken place in services, certain areas of manufacturing—some of them traditionally important to Cleveland's economy—continued to perform well. Higher than average wages in Cleveland relative to national wage rates did not account for areas of job losses in manufacturing, as opposed to areas of job gains. In general, areas with good possibilities for new growth were identified (e.g., medical and health services), and strategies for protecting strengths in established areas recommended (e.g., training to assure a skilled industrial workforce; consulting and management training directed to small manu-

[44] Aaron S. Gurwitz and G. Thomas Kingsley, *The Cleveland Metropolitan Economy*, prepared for the Cleveland Foundation by the Rand Corporation (Santa Monica, Calif., 1982); available from the Rand Corporation, Santa Monica, CA 90406.
[45] Ibid., p. 38.

facturing firms). Other goals identified were training of minority candidates for jobs in durable goods industries and technical fields, where they were underrepresented, and establishment of a permanent institutional home for the database and computer model developed for Cleveland by Rand. As the summary of the study's findings pointed out, a permanent location would increase the ability to translate "observed or predicted changes in the U.S. and world economies into their effects on the Cleveland area economy." Thus the model could help serve public policy makers, it could help shape area initiatives with respect to state and national policy, and presumably it could be available to private firms, unions, and community groups.[46]

Job creation and retention issues were central to this study, as was concern for maintaining an environment that was attractive to the Cleveland SMSA's thirty eight corporate headquarters of firms that ranked in the one thousand largest industrial firms according to *Fortune* magazine. Those headquarters were credited with generating strong growth in employment. Their retention was seen to hinge on the availability of skilled clerical and information-processing personnel, adequate transportation linkages, and generally good quality of life (e.g., culture and recreation) in the area.

The Cleveland study was not designed to shed light on the issue of surplus value creation and appropriation. However, some approximation of the shape of social surplus production and extraction can be gleaned from it. Most notably, data are provided for value added per hour of work in the study area compared to national averages and to a Southern state group. Value added per production worker hour is a statistical measure designed to track changes in productivity in an industry. It is the sum of profits and the cost of manufacturing inputs except the cost of raw materials and intermediate goods used in producing the final goods of a firm. This figure is compiled for the U.S. *Census of Manufacturers* with considerable difficulty, and with obvious sources of distortion, such as variations in the allocation of profits in a multiplant firm. Ambiguities in data affect all areas of the country. Cleveland—both the city and the SMSA—are shown to have higher than average U.S. value added per production hour, although

[46] Ibid., p. xx. The composition of the Advisory Committee for the Cleveland Foundation Rand Project contained among its twenty-four members one representative from a labor union. No representatives from community-based organizations seemed to be members. Ibid., appendix A, p. 217.

the gap was closing in the later years of the 1967–77 period studied. Between the years 1972 and 1977 the comparative amount of new investment taking place in the Cleveland SMSA gradually deteriorated, compared with new investment nationally. Both increased, but the gain in the Cleveland area was slower.[47] In addition, a significant portion of the new investment in Cleveland was for pollution control equipment. While desirable on other grounds, it offers little or nothing in the way of gains in future productivity.

In addition to value added per hour of work and amount of new investment, a third factor must be considered to get a rough sense of surplus extraction: What was happening to wages in the period? Rand's study found high manufacturing wages in Cleveland, compared to wages of other metropolitan areas of similar size. High wages there were attributed to a high incidence of durable goods manufacturing compared to other areas, the possibility of higher skill levels in the workforce, and the impact of a relatively high rate of unionization. Higher than average wages were being maintained in some sectors of the economy, but their incidence varied, and some manufacturing activities showed wages lower than the national average. Rand's researchers were unable to develop meaningful correlations between expanding areas of the economy and low wage rates or between declining areas and high wage rates.[48] High wages may keep a higher than average amount of new value created in the area in the form of workers' disposable income. If so, as it is spent, it has the usual beneficial multiplier effects for the local economy.

Assessing these three patterns of activity together, we can make only general observations about the flow of social surplus resulting from Cleveland area manufacturing activity. The most notable relationship among them is a consistently higher than average, if declining, value added per manufacturing hour and a dramatic decline in capital investment in manufacturing over the period of the study. With profits as a significant element of value added, social surplus during the study period was being extracted from, rather than put back into, the economy at a rate proportional to its creation. Decline in the rate of new investment, and particularly investment of the kind that will boost overall productivity, indicates a pattern that could leave Cleveland's economy in decline relative to the nation's.

[47] Ibid., pp. 107–11, 115.

[48] Ibid., pp. 60–73, and chap. 5.

From an analytical perspective, conclusions of this kind are maddeningly vague. After the high expenditures of time and resources for data-gathering and computer-based compilation, we are still far from saying anything very exact about social surplus. Fortunately, recent improvements over traditional input-output analysis in economic accounting techniques can provide a clearer picture of the generation and disposition of surplus.

Expanding Input-Output Analysis: The Monongahela National Forest Region Study

Input-output (I-O) tables represent economic accounts for an economy or a part of an economy. They provide information on the beginning and end points of basic economic transactions. The social accounting matrix (SAM) adds institutions such as governments and households to the basic I-O matrix, and it can incorporate distinct social groups by race, gender, or income level. The development of SAM enables fuller analysis of distributional implications of changes in an economy.

This development has progressed gradually since its introduction in 1961 by another Nobel laureate, Richard Stone. One of its most advanced regional applications in the United States, funded by the U.S. Forest Service,[49] is called the Impact Analysis System for Planning (IMPLAN). IMPLAN has been designed to improve substantially the availability of information for the evaluation of new projects undertaken on federal land. Its novel features include the ability to develop input-output matrices for geographic areas as small as a county. And rather than simply tracing materials flows, the technique can trace income payments from firms and organizations to those who receive them, separated into income levels. By linking the social accounting matrix to an income distribution matrix that provides information not only on wage and salary distribution from work but also estimates of income derived from property ownership, the result gives a detailed estimate of distributional aspects of changes in the economy.[50]

[49] Adam Rose, Brandt Stevens, and Gregg Davis, *Natural Resource Policy and Income Distribution* (Baltimore, Md., 1988). A brief history of the development of the social accounting matrix is presented on pp. 35–37 of their book. The work of Rose, Stevens, and Davis refines earlier work using social accounting matrices in evaluation of development projects by international agencies. See, for example, Clive Bell, Peter Hazell, and Roger Slade, *Project Evaluation in Regional Perspective* (Baltimore, Md., 1982).

[50] Rose, Stevens, and Davis, chap. 6. The authors develop a dividend distribution matrix

Economic accounting methodologies are most fully developed and best known for computing national income accounts and gross national product. They take as their basis primary data collected by government agencies at all levels of economic activity. The theoretical foundation for use of the data is usually a general equilibrium, market model. Aggregated data are computed in an additive accounting process, using double-entry balancing and control totals as tests for accuracy. Statistical methods may be used for estimating missing data or adjusting for insufficiently complete data, but in general this technique is based on real data, not econometric estimates.[51]

In order to obtain reasonably accurate projections of the distributional impact of projects to the outcome of I-O models, IMPLAN authors Adam Rose, Brandt Stevens, and Gregg Davis had to wrestle with different ways of theorizing income distributions. They found a post-Keynesian approach developed primarily in the work of Nicholas Kaldor to be most appropriate to their task and their I-O framework. In accepting that savings-consumption and factor payment patterns differ among social classes, they recognized structural aspects of distribution more fully than is usually the case in economics. Institutional factors, including property ownership patterns, governmental policy, and the role of labor unions, were also addressed in their model. Much of their effort was directed toward estimating the influence of environmental and natural resource outcomes of economic activity for a region. Refined and made more widely useable with appropriate software, this analysis could allow planners and citizen groups to evaluate the amount and proportion of wage and nonwage income to be generated by a project, as well as to estimate its multiplier effects in the region. For instance, it offers the ability, by incorporating patterns of capital ownership in its data, to determine the proportion of nonwage income that is retained and respent in the locality.[52] Estimates of this sort would enhance citizens' ability to choose among alternative forms of investment and to better plan for their region's future health.

---

from New York Stock Exchange survey data that adds new information to the social accounting matrix.

[51] Ibid., p. 38. The work of economic accounting is largely "deterministic" or based on the tabulation of actual data, in contrast to "inferential" statistical techniques such as econometrics.

[52] Ibid., pp. 12–17, 18.

Rose, Stevens, and Davis present several indexes designed to serve as quantitative measures of the distribution impact of projects. An individual impact matrix assesses direct economic effects, indirect ones, and what economists like to call market externalities, such as pollution, the aesthetic loss of open land, or traffic congestion. This matrix originates from a simulation that separates the direct income payments of each sector of the I-O matrix by the income group of the recipients. Externality "losses" are estimated by sectors. The result is a matrix showing gains and externality losses across sectors and income groups in dollars. The authors then convert the information into a single statistic, which they label the community impact index. It serves as an indicator of how a change in the economy affects, in qualitative terms, the majority of a community's population. This aggregation of the individual impact matrix into a summary figure represents the relative proportion of those who lose or gain by the change.[53]

The study details the authors' techniques for devising income distribution matrices that account for wage, salary, and property income distribution. Their pioneering work on income to property uses national data and assumes it will reflect regional patterns of distribution. They regionalize their social accounting matrix model by applying it to the Monongahela National Forest in West Virginia. Made up of portions of ten counties, this area of private, state, and federal land had a population in 1983 of approximately 200,000. Coal mining accounted for 39 percent of its total personal income. Income distribution coefficients, computed across ten income categories for fifty sectors of the economy, established distributional profiles. For example, the authors were able to demonstrate that in surface coal mining approximately 15 percent of generated income went to the two lowest categories of personal income in the distribution (under $5,000 and $5,000-9,999), while approximately 9 percent went to the two highest income categories ($75,000–99,999 and over $100,000) in 1982 dollars.[54] The lower categories, of course, contain far more individuals than the higher categories. This segment of their modeling had not been adjusted to take account of income flowing into and out of the region. While the model could be adjusted to

[53] Ibid., pp. 26–28, 29–30, 97–102.

[54] Ibid., chaps. 4–7 and pp. 85, 88, 90–91.

account for inflows and outflows of wages and salaries, data for income to property ownership are even more difficult to obtain on a regional basis than nationally.

Rose, Stevens, and Davis used their model to estimate the distributional impacts of a possible increase in coal surface mining in this national forest. They simulated the impact of a doubling in final demand for coal in their input-output table to estimate gross gains and losses and to assess their distribution. Potential damages were much more evenly spread (i.e., regressive in impact) than income gains, which were concentrated in upper income categories. Overall, the increase in surface mining led to more income, but slightly more adverse income distribution for the regional economy. A bare majority of individuals suffered a net loss if the proposed change was enacted. When alternative scenarios were tested in order to estimate income to capital that might leave the region, and the distribution of new jobs created for unemployed workers versus overtime for employed workers, all of the possible scenarios led to a reduction in the number of citizens that received net gains from the strip mining.[55]

Several problems with the analysis present themselves. They range from theoretical and methodological issues[56] to the very pragmatic, among which are the usual hurdles of data collection and computation. Few planning offices or citizen groups have staff members who are familiar with I-O and are willing, or able to do the work to expand it into a social accounting format. Such expertise can be hired. The labor intensive process of assembling and checking data and devising reasonable estimates for missing pieces takes skill and resources. And some data, such as the disposition of income to property, are simply difficult to obtain. An estimate, or a range of estimates, may have to provide the basis for educated conjecture about the ultimate distributional impact of new investment, or a loss of investment, for a community or region. However, the analysis allows for more careful estimation of the full impact on income of jobs created, new wage and salary income, and income to capital than has previously been possible.

[55] Ibid., pp. 101–3.

[56] These include the question of whether the authors' use of the term "class" in "income classes" carries any meaning beyond that of ordinal ranking and whether the positive-normative duality they suggest for economics is valid. Ibid., pp. 21, 31–32.

This survey of urban and regional economic studies indicates that valuable information can be made available to citizens, planners, and decision makers, but often at considerable cost. Private sector decision makers may find it of great enough benefit to them to fund a part of it, as in the case of the Cleveland Foundation study by Rand. Studies of the kind done by Rose, Stevens, and Davis raise distributional issues and are more politically sensitive. Funding for them is more likely to come from public sources or from citizen action groups. Studies supported at any level by public funds, whether through state or local government, federal grants, or state or federal support of universities, should contain not only the provision that results be made public but also a plan for making the public aware of their existence.

We cannot presume that area economic studies will be done with accounting categories that include social surplus or surplus value. Still, as we have shown, approximations of the surplus produced by an economy can be derived from basic data on value added or by working from data on income to property. Flows out of a neighborhood or region can be estimated by careful attention to consumer spending patterns, ownership patterns of business assets and property, and the rental flows activity of financial institutions.

The Macroeconomy

We have used the terms "social surplus" and "surplus value" to refer to the result of production that becomes income accruing to capital holders. But income to capital represents the tip of a much larger iceberg. The U.S. economy produces enormous amounts of social surplus and then squanders it by creating a large number of necessary but not very useful jobs. They serve primarily to sell products and channel surplus to capital owners. The nature and magnitude of the phenomenon require elaboration. In this final section of our discussion of social surplus we expand the scope of analysis to the national arena, and we expand the concept of social surplus beyond a narrow conception of categories of income to property. This work draws heavily on analysis of growth, accumulation, and unproductive activity in the macroeconomy by Edward Wolff.[57] Wolff not only

[57] Edward N. Wolff, *Growth, Accumulation and Unproductive Activity: An Analysis of the Postwar U.S. Economy* (New York, 1987).

provides important insight into how late twentieth-century capitalism works, but his work augments our understanding of the nature of local, public activity, to which we will turn in Chapter 6.

Compared to earlier economic systems, capitalism initially channeled dramatically higher proportions and magnitudes of surplus into productive activity. Less of society's surplus maintained an idle ruling class; more was devoted to production. Productivity skyrocketed, and where labor gained the ability to organize and fight for a larger share of the product, real wages rose. Capitalism could deliver the goods because of competitive pressure, including labor's pressure for higher wages, forcing continually new investment in more productive activity. Competition lowered the unit cost of output by combining more machinery with each unit of labor. Changes in the nature of capitalism have diminished its ability to put social surplus to productive use. Resources that were once poured into research and development, engineering departments, and new capital equipment have increasingly been diverted to legal departments, product management teams in marketing, and corporate take-overs. Circulation has become the dominant arena, and finance capital has gained a more prominant role in a new business hierarchy.[58]

What now constitutes rational economic behavior for individual firms does not produce the formerly beneficial result of raising productivity for the system as a whole. Much of private economic activity is now concerned with realizing and dividing social surplus, not producing it. Wolff's conclusions stem from careful inquiry into the magnitude of unproductive labor in the economy and its implications for economic growth.

Unproductive activity contributes to neither goods and services that people can enjoy nor to improvements and growth in capital stock.[59]

[58] For an overview of these changes, see Richard B. Du Boff, *Accumulation and Power: An Economic History of the United States* (Armonk, N.Y., 1989). The underlying nature of the changes is one area of debate between the protagonists of each "school" of Marxist analysis (chapter 1, note 16). For an institutional analysis that calls attention to corporate economic planning and the growing role of finance capital in that process, see John R. Munkirs, *The Transformation of American Capitalism: From Competitive Market Structures to Centralized Private Sector Planning* (Armonk, N.Y., 1985).

[59] Wolff's analysis emphasizes the supply side of the economy, in contrast to Paul A. Baran and Paul M. Sweezy, *Monopoly Capital: An Essay on the American Economic and Social Order* (New York, 1966), which uses a combination of Keynesian and Marxist analysis to develop a demand-side picture of surplus and waste in the U.S. economy. Wolff argues that the U.S. economy underwent a sharp increase in unproductive activity in the late 1940s

It curtails future growth. What institutions engage in unproductive labor? Common misconceptions lead us to think that government activity is unproductive, while private sector activity is productive. Some truth exists in that presumption, but much is erroneous as well. Similarly, analysts often presume that productive activity is involved in creation of goods, rather than services. Again, this thinking skirts the issue. In capitalist economies, productive activity creates both use value and exchange value, and it contributes to creation of surplus value. Surplus value is generally used in three ways. It provides for the consumption of segments of society in surplus-consuming class positions (e.g., capitalist consumption, income to rentiers), it is used for new capital formation, and it pays for unproductive activity. Unproductive activity creates neither exchange value nor use value; it simply absorbs social surplus.

What about the two forms of popular misconceptions cited above? Governments clearly provide use values (roads, public transit) that can be paid for in part or full on a fee-for-use basis (tolls, bus fare) that reflect exchange value. Firms provide services, such as moving people or goods or serving food, which have clear use and exchange value. Pointing to Western European examples of publicly owned firms engaged in making and selling products, Wolff argues that it is not the form of ownership that matters, but expanded reproduction from surplus value over time.[60] Thus, many public, quasi-public, and not-for-profit organizations create surplus value on an expanding basis. Other government services, such as education, are paid for indi-

---

and 1950s, and that change set the stage for the lower profitability, slower accumulation, and slower growth of the post-1960s.

Wolff uses Karl Marx's second definition of productive and unproductive activity from vol. 2, chap. 6, of *Capital*. These two concepts have sparked intense debate in political economy, with Marx, Adam Smith, and Joseph Schumpeter a few of its principal participants. For Wolff, "expenses of circulation are unproductive, where circulation is understood to refer to the selling of goods and services and the transferring of titles to and claims on productive output. Productive activity creates both use value and exchange value and hence commodities. Unproductive activity affects the disposition of commodities but creates neither use value nor exchange value" (Wolff, p. 38). Classifying productive and unproductive activity for any economy is contentious. Wolff identifies unproductive labor by sector or industry and by occupation, indicating debatable areas and arguments for the classification decisions that he makes. His estimates of the magnitude of unproductive activity in the U.S. economy are generally consistent with prior estimates of the same kind, but he uses more rigorous and detailed analysis to attain them.

[60] Ibid., p. 39.

rectly through tax assessments, and they have a priced, private market correlation. Hence, government services that provide identifiable use values can be classified as productive activities.

One measure of unproductive, surplus-absorbing activity in the economy can be found in statistics that assess the percentage absorption of surplus value by final demand components in economic activity. By Wolff's estimate of this measure, approximately two-thirds of surplus value was absorbed as unproductive labor time.[61] An economy that can devote only a third of its surplus labor time to reproducing its current standard of living has tremendous potential for growth or for reduction in work time for all. However, that promise is lost when surplus labor is largely used to prop up the system and assure its pattern of distribution.

Wolff's data also draw particular attention to the smallest and generally declining component of uses of surplus, the percentage of surplus value devoted to productive net capital formation or new investment. This figure ranged as high as 6.2 percent in the years after World War II and dropped to less than 2 percent in the mid-1970s.[62] As net capital formation diminishes, so does the ability to generate greater surplus in the future.

Unproductive activity increased in the post-war years in three important areas: business services, particularly those of advertising and legal services; defense spending within the federal government; and state and local government. While spending by state and local governments has increased, their portion of expenditures on goods and services deemed unproductive ranged from a fifth to a quarter, while for the federal government it was consistently over three quarters of expenditures.[63] Major components of productive activity at the state and local level are services such as sewage and sanitation, education, health and hospital services, highways, and fire protection. Far from being the sinkholes of waste that they are often purported to be in contemporary ideology, state and local government is, by Wolff's measure, using roughly three-quarters to four-fifths of its expenditures on directly usable goods and services. Their contrast with private sector waste is dramatic. Why is this so, and what are the implications?

[61] Ibid., pp. 135–36.
[62] Ibid., p. 136.
[63] Ibid., table 2.3, p. 49.

State and local governments face constant citizen pressure to justify and contain spending in order to limit taxes. More fundamentally, they deliver goods and services that are planned and for which resources are carefully allocated. Private sector activity is oriented to production for market exchange, where realization is uncertain. The output of firms large and small must be sold, or no surplus can accrue. Large amounts of resources must be expended in the effort to assure sale of product. And once that transaction is consumated, any surplus realized becomes the object of distributional contests. Wasteful forms of competition (in contrast to its productive form from the textbook market model and capitalism's heyday) and protection of claims to property become dominant activities.

Economic development could be served by carefully formulating strategies to provide more in the way of basic needs at the state and local levels of public sector activity. In addition, should communities and local governance units want to expand their activities into broader provision of goods and services, they could do so in ways that outshine the record of new capital formation established by the private sector in this country during the past half-century. Government spending has often been blamed for draining resources from the private sector and thus stifling investment. The assertion contains some truth, particularly in federal spending for defense. Given, however, that defense-related industries feed at the public trough in a host of ways that allow them to escape market discipline, business opposition to government spending in this arena has been limited. Business rhetoric has identified government in general as the monkey on the back of the private sector. The real causes of a stagnant economy lie in the private sector itself, and in the very logic of its late twentieth-century activities.

Local public sector activity is rational; it delivers goods and services with less waste than does the federal government (encumbered with the defense burden) or much of the private sector. Social surplus put to use in this arena—in improved transportation or education, for instance—could improve the performance of the U.S. economy. Local governments, along with community development corporations, not-for-profit corporations, and variations on these nonprivate-sector entities, can be used as engines of local surplus creation while they deliver goods and services. Two additional beneficial outcomes can result. First, surplus that remains in the public sector can be purposefully put to use on the basis of democratically determined choices. Second, rather than being "exported" by wealthy local capitalists or by distant or transnational corporations, the surplus remains in the area. There it can provide a foundation for local economic development.

We return to public sector issues in Chapters 5 and 6. There our focus will remain largely on local economics, rather than the macroeconomic arena.[64] Prior to that investigation, we will explore alternatives to either private or public sector-centered accumulation.

[64] Proposals for public sector initiatives at the national level can be found in Martin Carnoy and Derek Shearer, *Economic Democracy: The Challenge of the 1980s* (Armonk, N.Y., 1980), chap. 2. Their national proposals appear bolder than many others in their book, or in Carnoy, Shearer, and Russell Rumberger, *A New Social Contract* (New York, 1983). Perhaps a decade of "privatization" makes any call for public ownership appear bold.

3

Alternative Institutions of Accumulation: Gaining Financial Resources

In the next four chapters we investigate what can be done with social surplus locally. Our concern is that it be put to use in ways that hasten development and in ways that encourage democratic control over its disposition. In each chapter we provide profiles of organizations that, to some extent at least, achieve these goals. Some do so in contradictory ways, as they obviously reflect elements of the world in which they are created. We will generally sketch only one institution of a type and not argue that it has been chosen for close fit to some predetermined ideal. Other organizations similar to these examples exist, and we would like to see the creation of thousands more. Volumes could be written about how each could be improved and variations on them devised. From our perspective, the process of refining them as community-based generators of development will take place if, or when, they become more a part of our economy and society.

Our label "alternative" is most easily explained in comparison with "normal" institutions of accumulation in the economy. We use "alternative" to distinguish a broad terrain between private institutions—most notably the individual and the conventional, for-profit corporation—and public institutions that derive their revenue from taxation. Between the two poles lies a heterogeneous mix of nonprofit corporations, cooperatives, and other institutions that will be discussed in this and the following chapter. We will argue that these institutions could play a greater role than they now do in fostering community-based accumulation.

What can alternative institutions of accumulation do with respect to local development? A nonexhaustive list reflects organizations that can:

—attract resources to the community and recycle them there,

—respond to the community because their governing bodies incorporate a majority of local citizens and make use of democratic decision-making processes, and

—aggregate and use social surplus in ways that encourage local development.

The last characteristic points to an array of ways in which organizations can contribute to development. By augmenting basic needs such as prenatal care and training in good nutrition or by expanding people's capacity to participate in the processes of public decision making, they can contribute to human development. Or they may act more directly in economic development by providing physical infrastructure, training for work, or encouraging local businesses. Accumulation in alternative institutions can meet many objectives, but some of them may not lead to development in the community. For instance, accumulation may provide high salaries for staff members, which may serve local development only through trickle-down spending, or local accumulation may funnel social surplus out of the community to parent organizations. Local nonprofit institutions may decide to build secure asset portfolios by using their income for part or all of their operating budgets. In that case the organizations' work in the community can aid development, but their financial resources may not be put to work there. If portfolio resources are from outside the community, then whatever the organizations contribute to development is, for the community, net gain. On the other hand, if a large part of their funding is drawn from local social surplus, as in the case of a religious or service organization, then calculation of their net contribution to development is more complicated. The calculation must weigh factors as difficult to measure as the sense of shared community instilled by a local church, temple, or mosque against the local cost of supporting the staff, program, and building used to reach that sense of community.

Alternative institutions can also be defined in terms of their objectives with respect to social change. Many are organized simply to provide services that are lacking in a community; their goal is to survive from year to year in order to do their work. Others are intended to be, or they become, oppositional in character.[1] They shape

[1] Distinctions between alternative and oppositional organizations are developed in David

themselves on the premise that they must be more than ameliorative institutions; they work to change the balance of power and distribution of the fruits of life in their communities. Some do it through confrontation, and others by forging organizations that they believe will be prefigurative of a more humane social order and by urging others to follow their lead. As will be clear, the alternative institutions discussed here exhibit a mix of these characteristics.

Categories of institutions with the potential to contribute to local development are not hard and fast. For instance, we have included philanthropic organizations—generally private and rarely community-based or democratically run—because they have been a principal institutional means of transferring privately held surplus to public development projects. In the next chapter we include workers' cooperatives; they too are private organizations, but they are usually community-based and democratically managed.

Access to Money

Money is value in liquid form, and by definition communities in need of development need this resource. Human development, new community infrastructure, and business investment all require access to money. Its availability and sources, its cost to borrow or raise as a donation, and the income stream that it can generate are at issue. Here we take as given—for the moment—the distribution of wealth and investigate what has and can be done to provide financial resources for community-based developmental activity.

Regional superbanks and the international consolidation of the financial services industry should not make us nostalgic for the small-town bank. Local control of a savings institution is not a sufficient condition for maintaining community access to capital. The small-town bank was often run as an exporter of local savings. Managed ultraconservatively, it made money by funneling assets into the national banking system at rates that assured a profitable spread over the interest paid on local savings.

Moberg, "Experimenting with the Future: Alternative Institutions and American Socialism," in *Co-ops, Communes and Collectives*, John Case and Rosemary Taylor, eds. (New York, 1979). We first encountered the term used this way in Raymond Williams, "Base and Superstructure in Marxist Cultural Theory," in *New Left Review*, no. 83 (1973), pp. 3–16.

Services such as home mortgages are of concern to people who have achieved some level of financial success and stability in their lives. But many people are simply looking for a financial institution through which they can carry on many of the basic transactions of life: cash paychecks, save, pay bills, or finance consumer purchases. Institutions that want their business are becoming scarce. Deregulation of the banking industry as well as attempts to save failing thrift institutions in the 1980s added to the industry's centralization and concentration. Competition among regional banks has led to interest-bearing checking accounts and other gains for consumers, but these gains have been accompanied by new costs for many bank services. Thrift institutions have squeezed their least profitable (typically low-income, high transaction cost) customers. Low-income workers and retirees on social security still have checks to cash and bills to pay. The growing need for services for low-income citizens and a desire to keep and recycle assets in a community have helped inspire growth in credit unions. We will review gains in community-based finance through this institutional mechanism first.

Credit Unions

Credit unions are not-for-profit, tax-exempt institutions designed to meet the saving and borrowing needs of a distinct membership. The number of credit unions in the country has diminished in the past two decades, while their cumulative assets and membership have soared.[2] The 1980s brought bank and savings-and-loan failures, but dramatic success for credit unions. Credit unions are the co-ops of the financial world; they are run by boards of directors elected by depositors, rather than investor-owners, as in a bank.

Members of a credit union share a defining bond, such as being employees of the same firm, university, or hospital. The special category of community development credit unions (CDCUs) is of particular relevance to this study because it consists of credit unions designed to serve a community's specific needs, such as development of housing or minority-owned businesses. Approximately one hundred CDCUs now operate in the United States. They range in size

[2] Nathaniel C. Nash, "Clouds on Credit Union Horizon," *New York Times*, May 31, 1989.

from new store-front start-ups to the First American Credit Union in Window Rock, Arizona. First American, formerly Navajoland Credit Union, serves anyone who lives or works on an American Indian reservation in the state, and its assets are in the neighborhood of $20 million.

Santa Cruz Community Credit Union

Santa Cruz, California, launched its credit union in 1977 in a location adjacent to an emergency food bank. A sign in the window proclaimed goals of democratic management, recirculation of members' savings within the county, and community development lending. The credit union chose geographic area as its organizational definition and its members' common bond. It affiliated with and was assisted by the National Federation of Community Development Credit Unions.[3]

The Santa Cruz Community Credit Union (SCCCU) set out to distinguish itself in other ways as well. The principal lending activity of many credit unions is consumer goods loans, especially for automobiles. SCCCU members wanted to deemphasize consumer loans and concentrate a majority of their lending on community development projects, especially locally owned, cooperatively managed businesses. That proved a tough objective to meet.

Alternative business organizations share with most new small businesses problems of undercapitalization, inexperienced management, and troublesome start-up years. In addition they often carry the burden of new organizational forms, nonhierarchical structures, and democratic management practices. Bankers seeking to avoid risk can find numerous reasons not to lend to them. SCCCU sought these alternative business customers, provided them with financial advice, and made significant early loans to businesses such as a worker-owned print shop and a Hispanic strawberry production co-op.[4] For indi-

[3] John Isbister, "A Credit Union for the Community: The Santa Cruz Community Credit Union," undated photocopy (Santa Cruz, Calif.), pp. 1, 3–4. The National Federation of Community Development Credit Unions (59 John Street, 8th Floor, New York, NY 10038) provides technical assistance and other services to members.

[4] SCCCU's early years were spent bringing its business practices up to par while maintaining its political ideals. It overcame initial difficulties with volunteer labor and outside grants. In a two-year period SCCCU tripled its assets, clearing the million dollar mark. By 1982 SCCCU was self-sufficient and growing rapidly. John Isbister, "The Santa Cruz Community Credit Union: Business versus Politics," undated photocopy (Santa Cruz, California), and ibid., p. 11.

vidual members, SCCCU reached out to low- and moderate-income residents, offering workshops on personal finance and the demystification of money.

In 1988 SCCCU made 115 business loans totaling $2.5 million;[5] the loans were credited with helping to create 84 new jobs and save 125 existing jobs. The credit union worked closely with the Santa Cruz Community Housing Corporation to enable residents of a mobile home park to convert to cooperative ownership and to establish a low-income housing co-op. It also worked with the Housing Corporation on an eighty-unit, partly low-income, senior citizen housing project completed in 1987 in Santa Cruz. The deal involved HUD (Housing and Urban Development), the Teamsters' Pension Fund, and Christian Church Homes in construction of new, ocean-view units. By 1989 SCCCU's assets were over $10 million.

Credit unions are not immune from some of the pressures facing traditional banks. The board of SCCCU wrestled with the problem of low-balance, high-transaction-cost members' accounts. Finally they rejected a membership committee recommendation to raise the minimum balance to $100.[6] In its business lending, SCCCU staff members know they are filling a void in the local market. Banks often do not want to be bothered with the $10,000 to $25,000 loans that the credit union tends to make. For about the same transaction costs, they would prefer to make commercial loans of $50,000 or more.[7] Still, this credit union is committed to lower income borrowers and minority-owned businesses. Recognizing that the city of Santa Cruz is located in the county's wealthier northern area, it is expanding its activity southward to Watsonville. It has increased its lending in agricultural production and processing there.

Santa Cruz's credit union takes part in the Capitalization Program of the Federation of Community Development Credit Unions, which is a vehicle for attracting funds from major national philanthropic, religious, and service organizations. These funds are sometimes deposited directly with the credit union at the current interest rate and sometimes loaned to them at low rates of interest. The funds expand the asset base of the credit union and enable it to make more loans.

[5] Santa Cruz Community Credit Union, *Newsletter* (Winter 1989), p. 4.

[6] Ibid., p. 2.

[7] Interview with Jeff Wells, vice president for loans and community development, SCCCU, Santa Cruz, California, March 17, 1989.

Credit unions thus act as magnets attracting segments of national pools of social surplus.

The Caja Laboral Popular

We will briefly step outside our domestic context to describe one European financial institution. To our knowledge, it is unique in scale of operation and connection to cooperative production and regional economic development in a Western market economy. The Caja Laboral Popular is one of the central institutions in the success story of the Mondragon network of cooperatives in Basque Spain. The first of Mondragon's many industrial co-ops was founded in 1956, and the Caja Laboral in 1959. Created as a savings institution for the Basque provinces, it also is a lending institution to help finance workers' co-ops. Its assets in 1987 totaled close to $3 billion.[8]

The Caja Laboral Popular is a second-degree or superstructural co-op in the Mondragon system; it exists to serve the worker-controlled co-ops. Its own workers hold one-third of the seats on its board of directors, and the co-ops that it serves elect the other two-thirds. A contract of association must be signed by each co-op linked to the Caja. By specifying the working relationship between the Caja and its member co-ops, the contract maintains the character of the Mondragon system.[9]

The credit union operation of the Caja Laboral Popular has close to two hundred retail branches spread throughout the Basque provinces.[10] Deposits are available for financing industrial, service, and consumer co-ops in the Mondragon system. They are put to use in the region rather than being funneled out of the relatively depressed Basque lands for use in other growth areas of the Spanish economy, or out of Spain for use in other parts of Europe.

The Caja is an amalgam of several kinds of banking institutions. In addition to the typical saving-consumer loan function of a credit

[8] Caja Laboral Popular, *Annual Report 1987* (Guipuzcoa, Spain, 1988), p. 46. An exchange rate of 115 pesetas to one U.S. dollar was used for converting assets of 339 billion pesetas.

[9] The best English language summary of the history, organizational form, and scope of the Mondragon co-ops is Caja Laboral Popular, *The Mondragon Experiment* (Guipuzcoa, Spain, 1987). An accessible recent source in the U.S. is William Foote Whyte and Kathleen King Whyte, *Making Mondragon: The Growth and Dynamics of the Worker Cooperative Complex* (Ithaca, 1988). See particularly chaps. 8 and 15 on the Caja Laboral Popular.

[10] Caja Laboral Popular, *Annual Report 1987*, p. 54.

union, it is an investment bank for the co-ops of the system, and it has an entrepreneurial division that provides technical assistance and planning services to new co-ops in the process of forming and to co-ops in need of reorganization or rejuvenation. The Caja was intended to be a development bank for job creation in cooperative enterprises. Its activities have expanded into research on the Basque, Spanish, and European economies, into elements of urban and industrial planning, and into consulting to its members. The studies or economic research section of the Caja is now closely linked to the Basque regional government's economic surveys and planning for development.[11] With approximately eighteen thousand jobs in eighty six industrial co-ops and many more in its consumer, social security, education, and housing cooperatives,[12] the Mondragon network is a dynamic developmental force. At the center is what could have been a simple credit union, but became a unique and sophisticated cooperative bank for regional development.

In magnitude of money, a local credit union may provide small gain for a community. However, community-based credit unions keep savings in the community and under local control. They allow a part of savings to be put back to work at a more modest rental rate than a loan company would impose, and they pay the interest out to members who reside in the community. Checking (share draft) services are available; checks can be cashed without paying exhorbitant fees; members have a voice in running the institutions. In principle and practice, these are major gains over bank branches that would take savings and deny loans or that price services out of reach of low-income patrons. Their increasing ability to service new businesses and nonprofit organizations makes them valuable additions in development of alternatives to conventional firms. Credit unions can also attract outside savings, they bring together human resources and skills, and they can serve as a focal point for planning and action for community development.

[11] From interviews with staff of the Area de Estudios, Division Empresarial, of the Caja Laboral Popular, June 29, 1988, and June 4, 1984.

[12] Figures are from the *Annual Report 1987*, p. 64. In 1987 the Mondragon system included a consumer co-op, Eroski, employing approximately sixteen hundred people regionally, fifteen housing co-ops, forty-six educational co-ops (from elementary schools to a polytechnic institute), eight agricultural co-ops, and nine service and support co-ops, including a healthcare system serving over forty-six thousand people (pp. 72–85).

Community Development Loan Funds

Needs that inspired groups to form credit unions have also inspired more recent developments in community-based finance. Revolving loan funds engage in lending similar to community development credit unions, but they function independently of retail savings operations. Sometimes they simply bring together lenders and those actually engaged in community development efforts in need of funds. More commonly today, loan funds themselves manage a portfolio of borrowed capital. Community Development Loan Funds (CDLFs) borrow money and lend it at moderate rates of interest "to benefit communities and individuals denied sufficient access to traditional capital markets."[13] Loan funds are not-for-profit, tax-exempt corporations. Their capital base comes from loans made to them by charitable foundations, religious groups, individuals, and corporations.[14]

CDLFs began in the second half of the 1970s. The Cooperative Bank of New England, based in Hartford; Common Space Loan Fund and North Country Development Fund, both based in Minneapolis; the Fund for an Open Society in Philadelphia; and the Institute for Community Economics Revolving Loan Fund of Greenfield, Massachusetts, were all in operation by 1980. By 1988 thirty had become members of the National Association of Community Development Loan Funds (NACDLF), and seven funds were awaiting full membership when they reached full operation.[15] Other associates of NACDLF are either loan funds, lenders, or foundations committed to similar objectives, such as the National Cooperative Bank Development Corporation, the Trust for Public Land Property, and the Campaign for Human Development.

Most CDLFs have housing as a principal concern, others focus on business development, and many do both. The aim is to be responsible stewards of investment resources and to deliver them to low-

[13] National Association of Community Development Loan Funds, statement of purposes and activities (Greenfield, Mass., n.d.).

[14] Cascadia Loan Fund in Seattle and some other funds use a somewhat different method of operation. They organize investors who deposit funds in a credit union or local bank, and those funds serve as collateral for loans from the financial institutions to borrowers approved by the sponsoring fund. See "New Community Loan Funds around the Country," *Community Economics* 8 (Spring 1985), 2.

[15] National Association of Community Development Loan Funds, *Profile of Member Fund Activity* (Greenfield, Mass., June 30, 1988).

income, unemployed, and otherwise economically disenfranchised people. The activities of NACDLF's members are assisting those who most need capital, engaging those who have capital, and encouraging those who manage it, with the objective of increasing the flow of capital to projects that meet community needs. The thirty NACDLF members had acted on these objectives to the extent of over $20 million in current loans by mid-1988.[16]

Many CDLFs focus on specific geographic areas, and some assist a particular form of development. The Industrial Cooperative Association Revolving Loan Fund assists workers' cooperatives and worker-owned businesses nationally. The loan fund of the Association for Regional Agriculture Building the Local Economy (ARABLE), based in Eugene, Oregon, serves a three-county area to encourage small farmers who produce food for the local market. A loan fund developed by the Fund for Southern Communities in Atlanta was initiated in conjunction with the South Atlanta Land Trust (SALT), discussed in Chapter 4. A number of funds target traditional small business development (e.g., The Delta Foundation/Rural Development Loan Fund in Greenville, Mississippi; Coastal Enterprises, Inc. in Wiscasset, Maine), and others encourage self-employment (e.g., Micro Industry Credit Rural Organization [MICRO] in Tucson, Arizona, and the Women's Self-Employment Project in Chicago).[17] In many cases, CDLFs and their more specialized versions act as retailers of credit, or low-cost credit, from funds provided by large foundations.

Community loan funds face a number of hurdles. Low-income families attempting to buy their first house, small-scale specialty farmers, and new cooperative businesses send most lenders running for cover. Loan fund staff members have to provide technical advice, broker deals with other possible lenders, serve as advocates, and still keep cool, analytical heads. An early and informal estimate of loss rates for CDLFs was seven-tenths of one percent, somewhat higher than for commercial banks of less than $10 billion in assets.[18] Loan funds maintain reserves for losses, and they protect lenders to the funds.

[16] NACDLF, statement; *Profile*.

[17] Laura Henze, Nancy Nye, and Richard Schramm, *Summary Report*, Roundtable Workshop for Business Development and Self-Employment Loan Funds Serving Low Income People, Tufts University Center for Management and Community Development (October 1, 1988).

[18] Scott Bronstein, "A New Lender of Last Resort," *New York Times*, December 1, 1985.

These lenders face the dilemma of what markup to impose on their loans. Not only do they make credit available to borrowers who might otherwise be denied loans, but they do so at lower than market rates of interest. Making loans at 5 to sometimes even 10 percentage points below what standard market rates would be makes a broader range of community based projects possible. It also means that CDLFs struggle to keep costs down. Many function with donated facilities and services and at least some volunteer labor.

CDLFs allow those with money to have their cake, and eat most of it too. Lenders retain claim on their assets but earn less than they could through other forms of investment. The difference in earnings, compared to investing or lending at an interest rate based on comparable risk, amounts to a charitable contribution to the loan fund's borrowers. From the vantage point of poorer communities, the funds can help stabilize or revitalize a community. Social surplus remains in the private realm, but it can fuel economic development in target areas.

Development Banks

Loan funds are one way of paring down the complexity of serving an array of communities' financial needs. Development banks are another. Typically not-for-profit corporations that accept federally insured deposits, development banks are created to service depressed areas or nontraditional borrowers. They deliver not only money but technical assistance and management training, acting as a bridge between private-sector capital and expertise and public-sector development programs.

Despite the 1977 Community Reinvestment Act (CRA) and its companion Home Mortgage Disclosure Act, poor neighborhoods continue to be poorly served by traditional banks.[19] These laws mandate that

---

Henze, Nye, and Schramm, *Summary Report*, p. 27, points to write-offs of 12 percent of invested capital from their sample of funds and indicates that this figure compares favorably with losses for public sector loan programs.

[19] For a very optimistic interpretation of the impact of the Federal Community Reinvestment Act, see James Carras, "Getting Your Money's Worth," in *Everybody's Business: A People's Guide to Economic Development*, *Southern Exposure* 14:5–6 (1986), 79–82. Local banks carry copies of their current CRA statements. For two recent indications of discrimination in bank lending, see Bill Dedman, "The Color of Money," *The Atlanta Journal and Constitution*, May 1, 1988; Allen R. Gold, "Racial Pattern Is Found in Boston Mortgages," *New York Times*, September 1, 1989.

banks meet credit needs at all levels of their community and bar lenders from "redlining," the practice of designating areas in their community where they withhold service because of race or income level of residents. Attorneys for community groups and legal services have been able to use the CRA to gain valuable information on lending practices. They can then use persuasion or legal leverage to gain fairer lending practices and specific commitments to mortgage, home improvement, and small business loans in low-income or largely minority neighborhoods.

Illinois Neighborhood Development Corporation

When the Illinois Neighborhood Development Corporation (INDC) took over South Shore Bank in Chicago, it did more than move into lending. INDC realized that distressed communities would not attract investment because they were perceived as presenting higher costs and risk and lower potential payoff than other possible investment sites.[20] This is the clear-eyed assessment of low-income neighborhoods in a profit-maximizing market economy. A community or neighborhood has to figure out how to absorb the costs, face the risks, and accept what may be a lower-than-market payoff.

Ronald Grzywinski and his colleagues at INDC, a federally regulated bank holding company, set out to raise money to launch their neighborhood revitalization project in 1972.[21] They found a neighborhood in South Chicago that was deteriorating but not in the depths of decay, and in it and on the market, South Shore National Bank.[22] Founders had a track record in reviving an ailing bank and in lending to minority entrepreneurs. They saw banks as having certain advantages compared to credit unions. First and most obviously, banks could be bought as "going" institutions. In telling the INDC story, Richard Taub also notes that banks are institutions that need no explanation and that have important symbolic value. They are centers of communication about economic activity in a community and are

[20] Ronald Grzywinski, "A Proposal to Create Permanent Neighborhood Development Banks," *The Entrepreneurial Economy* 3 (December 1984), 6–7.

[21] INDC was founded on Ronald Grzywinski's initiative, with the assistance of Milton Davis, Mary Houghton, and Jim Fletcher. See Richard P. Taub, *Community Capitalism* (Boston, 1988), pp. 17–18.

[22] South Shore is a community of approximately seventy-five thousand people on Lake Michigan, south of Chicago's commercial center. It contains several distinct neighborhoods, and its population is mostly African-American. Formerly a middle-class suburb of Chicago, it has undergone slow decline over several decades.

thought to be honest in monetary transactions. In August 1973 South Shore Bank was sold to INDC for $3.2 million. The bulk of the equity came from churches, foundations, and two socially concerned businessmen.[23] With a $2.4 million loan, South Shore came under the INDC umbrella as a highly leveraged bank.

Development activities were organized as nonbank subsidiaries of INDC; they brought to the company capacities that are not generally found working in close collaboration with a bank. Significant elements of the initial plans included a real estate development company concerned with both residential and commercial property; a social development subsidiary for cooperative housing and job training and placement; and a minority enterprise small business investment corporation (MESBIC) that could pump equity capital into the community's minority-owned businesses.

By 1986 South Shore had holdings of $119 million, of which $46 million were development deposits, funds attracted to the bank through marketing of its social development mission to socially conscious savers. South Shore largely invented this strategy.[24] By reaching out to organizations outside the community—pension funds, religious institutions, foundations—it built a larger lending portfolio with lower transaction cost than neighborhood deposits could provide. A development audit informed major savers about what their deposits had enabled the bank and its subsidiaries to do.

Evidence of the extent to which INDC was able to reach outside its community to bring capital to South Shore also exists on the equity side of the ledger, in its shareholder profile. INDC shareholders of record in March 1985 read like a *Who's Who* of liberal foundations and churches, including the John D. & Catherine T. MacArther Foundation, Charles Stewart Mott and Ford foundations, and the Episcopal Church and North Shore Unitarian Society. Allstate Insurance and Standard Oil of Indiana were also shareholders. Taub has described South Shore as a "broker between the community and the corporate world."[25] Its principals knew where the surplus was and worked effectively to move some of it into a run-down Chicago neighborhood, where it could help fuel revitalization.

Although South Shore Bank is the name associated with this successful revitalization, Grzywinski came to argue that what had been

[23] Taub, *Community Capitalism*, pp. 20–21.
[24] Ibid., pp. 63, 79.
[25] Ibid., pp. 78, 135.

accomplished might be done better in other communities without a retail bank. He advocated a strategy of neighborhood development banks, built on the INDC model, designed to attract public-spirited entrepreneurs for public and private projects as well as the large quantities of cash essential to the urban rebuilding effort.[26]

A bank holding company without a retail bank could avoid undercapitalization and be free of the high transaction costs associated with running a community bank or credit union. It could seek major deposits, say in $100,000 F.D.I.C.-insured certificates of deposit, from a wide range of depositors including corporations, pension funds, churches, state and local governments, and other organizations that had accumulated large amounts of liquid assets. Those funds would be converted to development credit, keeping the bank holding company well hedged against risk. Loans could be made at reasonable rates for housing and other residents' needs. New job opportunities could be filled by neighborhood residents whose skills were developed through a targeted training program. Other subsidiaries of the holding company could initiate commercial development in the area. The fact that the bank was regulated would help balance its advocacy role with its need to meet industry performance norms. This model was offered as a logical next step toward a better institutional vehicle for social investing and neighborhood rejuvenation.[27]

The development bank concept is being put to work in other parts of the country. One example stems from a credit union and technical assistance center in Durham, North Carolina.[28] The Center for Community Self-Help was established in 1980 to create and stabilize jobs in the state and to assist in creating housing in depressed rural areas. It quickly established a track record in helping to launch worker-owned businesses. The center then turned to establishing a credit union. Initial financing was from the sale of $17 in cakes baked by one of the worker-owned firms it had assisted. In three years, its assets topped $5 million.[29] The center has also set up a venture capital fund

[26] Grzywinski, "A Proposal," p. 7.
[27] Ibid.
[28] Another, the Southern Development Bancorporation, has been launched in rural Arkansas by the Winthrop Rockefeller Foundation. See National Center for Policy Alternatives Program Summary–Southern Development Bancorporation for Rural Development, NCPA, Washington, D.C., November 17, 1987.
[29] Jim Overton, "Own Your Own Job: The Center for Community Self-Help," *Southern Exposure* 14:5–6 (1986), 52–55.

to make equity investments in risky new businesses, and to enable it to move more quickly in assembling financial packages for worker take-overs of firms.

More recently, the center began work on a development bank. In its appeal to the North Carolina legislature for a $2 million appropriation to serve as loan reserves for the bank, the center made the following case. Foundations and corporations had been lined up to match the state appropriation on a 2-for-1 basis, yielding reserves, with initial seed money in place, of at least $6 million. Each dollar of development reserves supports development deposits of from five to ten dollars, making possible a minimum of $25 million in development loans; and since development loans have a repayment cycle of five to seven years, that $25 million fund would get recycled to new projects frequently. This is the argument for leveraging public funds for the sake of economic development. At the end of 1987, with only $4 million available in development funds, the center had helped save or create hundreds of jobs, it had made mortgage loans to over one hundred low-income, minority first-time homeowners, and assisted several employee-owned businesses, each with seventy to three hundred owner-workers.[30] Its aim is to do this work on a grander scale throughout the state.

Loan funds and development banking provide access to greater resources. They open an avenue by which people who oversee repositories of social surplus can, if so inclined, loan it out for use in poorer communities of the country. They get it back, generally augmented with something less than the going market rate of interest. Still, their "socially conscious investment" will have made resources available to communities starved for them. How much of the church endowment or the foundation portfolio retailed by loan funds or development banks originated in the poor communities selected for help would be difficult, but important, to determine.

Foundations and Philanthropic Organizations

Philanthropies and foundations are awkward additions to a chapter on alternative institutions of accumulation. They are not profit-

[30] Center for Community Self-Help/Self-Help Credit Union, "Development Banking in North Carolina," (Durham, N.C., 1988).

seeking corporations or government agencies, and they are clearly institutions of accumulation. On the other hand they are usually privately controlled and traditionally managed. While this is particularly true of foundations, some philanthropic organizations are under broader social control. In some respects both are mainstream organizations of accumulation, traditional complements to for-profit corporations and private individuals.

Two reasons compel us to discuss these organizations. The first is that they are repositories of very large amounts of social surplus. The second is that other alternative organizations frequently turn to them as sources of funding. We will explore these factors before considering other aspects of their operation and reviewing a specific case of the impact of philanthropic activity on a community.

Americans give over $100 billion per year to charitable organizations.[31] Individual donors generally account for over 75 percent of the annual receipts of charities, with bequests, foundations, and corporations making up the rest. Contributions are divided into the following approximate percentages: religious organizations, 48 percent; educational institutions, 12 percent; healthcare organizations, 10 percent; the arts and cultural organizations, 7 percent; and the remainder to other causes. Within these groups of organizations many, and especially religious organizations, pass funds to community-based activities and organizations.

Foundations are both a source of funds for charitable organizations and an important direct source for community-based organizations. The largest of them control massive amounts of social surplus. Their portfolios of investments (accumulated social surplus) generate a stream of income (current social surplus) that sustains their annual giving, staff salaries, and operating expenses. Measured by assets, the largest foundation is Ford. It operates on the stream of earnings from an approximately $5 billion investment portfolio. Other large foundations, those with over $2 billion in assets, include the J. Paul Getty Trust, the W. K. Kellogg Foundation, the MacArthur Foundation, the Lilly Endowment, and the Robert Wood Johnson Foundation.[32] Each foundation has an agenda for giving and lending its funds that includes specific target sectors or problems, sometimes geographic priorities,

[31] *Giving U.S.A.*, 34th ed., a report of the American Association of Fund-Raising Council's Trust for Philanthropy (New York, 1989).
[32] The Foundation Center, report on assets, 1988.

and possible restrictions concerning the type of organizations that they will fund. For community-based projects, foundations often provide start-up funds with the expectation that the donee will develop a regular, perhaps local, funding base for its activities.

Philanthropy now has a "new age" institutional form that targets community-based organizations and itself comprises a more area or regional orientation. The Haymarket People's Fund in Cambridge, Massachusetts, and Vanguard Fund in San Francisco were 1970s prototypes for liberal, community, and issue-oriented philanthropies. Founded by a young generation from wealthy families, most have included community activists on their grant-making committees. Today progressive community-based funds and several national charities are tied together in the Funding Exchange, a national coalition of donors. Their claimed common bond is "empowerment philanthropy" to eliminate inequality and injustice. In 1988 Funding Exchange members gave approximately $3 million to four hundred recipient organizations working on issues such as women's health, lesbian and gay rights, and housing for the poor.[33]

Philanthropic activity can take other institutional forms as well. For-profit corporations engage in it routinely, making contributions to the arts, educational institutions, and other causes. Contributions help lower the firm's tax bill, but they also represent social surplus that flows to public uses rather than directly to stockholders. Control over the flow rests, of course, in the hands of corporate decision makers. In an unusual case of corporate philanthropy by an unusual business venture, Ben and Jerry's Homemade, Inc., the ice cream makers, gives 7.5 percent of pretax profit to grass-roots, nonprofit organizations. Its Ben and Jerry's Foundation supports projects that are considered models of social change and creative problem-solving for human and community development.

A common argument is that foundation money is "tainted." Populist sentiments seem to be at the root of the idea that money amassed by the Fords, Rockefellers, or Mellons is a uniquely suspect form of surplus. From our perspective, this complaint muddies already murky water. All privately appropriated social surplus derives from the same source—people's present and past work. Foundations are a current

[33] Mary Nick-Bisgaard, "Funding Alternatives," *In These Times*, July 5–18, 1989; Kathleen Teltsch, "Young Philanthropists Give to Nontraditional Causes," *New York Times*, August 21, 1986.

repository of profits from capitalist enterprise, and as much of that money should be returned to poor communities and people as can be wrung from the foundations. The principal near-term concerns are what may be given up or compromised to get it, and at what point the organization seeking it says, "Thanks, but no." In the longer term, of course, the point is to see that such large amounts of social surplus do not come under private control.

Finally, considerable individual and business giving takes place through United Charities, as various United Way organizations are called. United Charities is a primary nongovernmental means by which social surplus is aggregated for use by community-based health and welfare organizations.[34] It has been the target of ongoing attack because of allegations that its support goes essentially to white and middle-class activities, and that its lock on individual giving through payroll deduction reduces other charities to nickel-and-dime and bake-sale fund-raising. Its local structural form creates potential for it to be forward-looking and innovative in meeting community needs; its cautious and often elite-controlled administration can undermine the promise to be more responsive to all community members.

Tupelo, Mississippi

Tupelo is located in the hill country of northeast Mississippi. Perhaps best known as the birthplace of Elvis Presley, this city of twenty-five thousand is an example of what local philanthropy and civic innovation can do for development.[35] Tupelo's corner of Mississippi is a poor one, yet Tupelo has a standard of living second in the state to Jackson, the capital.

The most prominent leader in Tupelo's remarkable history came to town in 1934. George McLean had been a student and teacher of philosophy, he was deeply religious, and he had the idea that a news-

[34] Current assessments of these organizations can be found in Carl Milofsky, ed., *Community Organizations: Studies in Resource Mobilization and Exchange* (New York, 1988). Chap. 6 of the collection, Susan Rose-Ackerman, "United Charities: An Economic Analysis," and chap. 7, Deborah Kaplan Polivy, "The United Way: Understanding How It Works Is the First Step to Effecting Change," provide mainstream analysis and bibliographic material on these charities. A more critical assessment of philanthropy can be found in Teresa Odendahl, *Charity Begins at Home: Generosity and Self-Interest among the Philanthropic Elite* (New York, 1990).

[35] Information on Tupelo's history and development comes from Dick Mendel, "Tupelo, Mississippi: A Glimmer of Light amid the Shadows in the Sunbelt," unpublished manuscript, Chapel Hill, N.C. (MDC, Inc., 1988); CREATE, Inc., summary statement (n.d.).

paper could be a catalyst for improving local economic and cultural life. He bought the bankrupt *Daily Journal* and soon annoyed local business people by championing wage increases for local workers and their unionization efforts. He was an early advocate for agricultural diversification in the area, using his editorial page to educate and cajole. After World War II he paid for a consultant's study of the area's economy. The study recommended a rural community development council (RCDC), designed to modernize agricultural practices, encourage diversification, and engage in community development. Support from businesses and civic clubs helped fourteen local councils emerge, and they were all encouraged and celebrated in the pages of the *Daily Journal*. By the 1950s, the Tupelo RCDC model became the centerpiece of the Eisenhower administration's rural development program.

Despite McLean's liberal views he was made head of the Chamber of Commerce. It established a community development foundation in 1948 that became much more than a means for enticing low-wage jobs into the area. It began doing everything possible to promote "the upbuilding of the community, including industry, agriculture trade, recreation, education, and other matters of civic interest."[36] Tupelo's three banks somewhat reluctantly joined with the *Daily Journal* as sponsors of the foundation, which has operated for over forty years and now has annual budgets in the range of a million dollars. Along with the rural community development councils, it has helped assure that this small city became the economic hub of its region.

To achieve that success, Tupelo also had to go through a transition to an industrial center. It attracted Rockwell International after raising half of the funds needed for new vocational training at a breakfast meeting of community leaders. Active recruitment attracted furniture makers and several new makers started and grew locally. Local leaders were cautious about relying too much on outside industries. As McLean put it, "Most money generated by these plants, other than the workers' salaries, doesn't stay here. It goes to the individual plant's main headquarters which are off in some other state."[37] He understood the economics of local development. He also understood development as more than economic in nature.

One of the attractions that Tupelo held out to potential new busi-

[36] Community Development Foundation, charter, 1948, quoted in Mendel, p. 14.
[37] Quoted in ibid., p. 16.

nesses was its commitment to civic development and education. Tupelo's anti-poverty agency, Lift, Inc., was organized by McLean. It provided the area's first Head Start program and public family planning clinics. Local donations helped build Tupelo's North Mississippi Medical Center into a large, modern hospital. Lee County was the first in Mississippi to integrate its school system. The Community Development Foundation and TVA assisted Itawamba Junior College to develop a vocational training curriculum that included robotics and automated manufacturing techniques. In the cultural arena, Tupelo is reputed to be the smallest city in the United States which maintains a metropolitan symphony. An arts festival assures the availability of more broadly popular art. In the 1970s McLean gave over a million dollars to the county school system for the purpose of adding a teacher's aide to all first-grade classrooms.

McLean capped his philanthropy by bequeathing all of his stock in the *Daily Journal* to the Christian Research, Education, Action, Technical Enterprise (CREATE). CREATE channels over a million dollars a year, both newspaper profits and other donations, to community projects in northeast Mississippi. Its aim is to sustain leadership development for progressive community activity and to enrich the health, education, and cultural lives of area residents. As a former Mississippi governor, William Winter, commented, McLean used his newspaper to "create a base of public opinion that supported creative economic development and progressive social attitudes."[38]

In addition to this citizen's foresight and leadership, two other factors stand out. One is that the *Daily Journal* was locally owned, so that the surplus it generated stayed in the area. The other is that its owner returned a substantial part of it to the community. While the institutions created from the surplus may have been controlled by a local elite, their resources aided local development in a state with a relatively underdeveloped public sector.

Nonprofit, tax-exempt charitable organizations attract funding on the basis of the individual choices of donors. Many of the goods and services they provide are close cousins of public goods funded through government tax revenue, but donors get to choose among a variety of competing organizations and their causes in allocating money.[39] In

[38] Quoted in ibid., p. 25.

[39] There is a significant "free-rider" problem inherent in organizations supported by vol-

general, the donor's payoff is the satisfaction derived from his or her gift.

Tax policy has encouraged this process by allowing donations to be itemized deductions from income in computing tax liability. However, the incentive has been accompanied by a clear class bias; it has been strongest for high-income taxpayers—those who tend to itemize deductions and face higher marginal tax rates. Recent tax reforms have reduced marginal tax rates, but also further narrowed people itemizing deductions to the wealthy.[40] Tax policy has increased existing incentive of charitable organizations to focus their appeals for funds on high-income individuals. Although this may be seen as an informal or voluntary form of progressive taxation, it is not. High-income individuals do not have to give, and in fact they give at rates that are lower, as a percentage of their income, than do some lower income groups.[41] Nevertheless, charitable and educational institutions have designed policies to appeal to this elite segment of the population, such as the practice of offering membership on the organizations' boards of directors. Democratic control is absent from the start, and tax policy further diminishes the probability that these organizations incorporate into their program design and policy-making people they ostensibly exist to serve.

A solution to this tax policy problem is certainly imaginable. Contributions to tax-exempt, nonprofit organizations could be deducted—in full or a percentage—directly from one's tax bill.[42] A ceiling would be needed to assure that these contributions could not be fully substituted for tax payments. As a tax credit, rather than an itemized deduction from income, all contributors would encounter the same after-tax impact. Alternatively, services offered by these organizations could also be provided, perhaps more efficiently, by the government through tax revenue.[43] However, tax credit for donations

---

untary donations. It gets less attention from conservatives than "free-rider" problems in government expenditures, no doubt because contributions to these organizations are a matter of individual choice, and not government "coercion."

[40] In the period from 1982–86 charitable contributions were deductible whether or not the taxpayer itemized deductions. That provision in the tax code was eliminated in the 1986 tax reform.

[41] Bureau of the Census, *Statistical Abstract 1988*, p. 359.

[42] See Burton A. Weisbrod, *The Nonprofit Sector* (Cambridge, Mass., 1988), pp. 164–65, for a discussion of the tax credit alternative to deductions from income for contributions to charitable organizations.

[43] A universal tax system eliminates the "free-rider" problem. Inefficiencies of government are controlled best at the local level, where most of these programs operate. Tax collection

allows citizens to tailor their support for some nongovernmental services and to enable the services to continue to be carried out in a way that often mobilizes local volunteers. If the tax credit reform was matched by a requirement for broadly representative and democratically structured governance for certification as a nonprofit, tax-exempt organization, then this segment of our social activity would be salvaged from a privileged status in largely private hands. Another portion of social surplus would be brought under more democratic control.

On a broader level, those favoring expanded federal, state, and local action must successfully reverse the tide of restriction on taxation and public spending. In all realms of taxation, progressivity must be restored to the final outcome. Paying a smaller percentage of income should be reserved for those who have the least, not those who can afford tax attorneys.

All of the institutions described here can help a community overcome some aspects of its money problems; none of them will solve its problems. They all address access to money, and a measure of the rough shape many communities are in is that a gain in access to capital can be seen as a significant victory.

Development banks, loan funds, and the community development aspect of credit union operation attract funds to communities, and they broker the funds that they receive. They use forms of local control that may or may not be democratic. The organizations that they create may be nondemocratic traditional firms in the private sector. Yet to the extent that development banks, loan funds, and community development credit unions function in conjunction with publicly controlled local development agencies, they can be important elements of a public process of planning and implementation for development.

---

is certainly more efficient than the costly, nonstop campaigns run by charitable and nonprofit organizations in the hope of getting contributions.

4

Alternative Institutions of Accumulation: Building Assets in the Community

Chapter 3 discussed institutions that help a community attract and retain financial resources. Based on the same criteria, we now turn to institutions that can directly fulfill local development objectives. Attracting resources to the community and keeping them there, offering the potential—at the least—for local and democratic control, and aggregating social surplus for use in local development remain central concerns. But financial assets do not sit in vaults; value in liquid form gets put to work. Here we focus on more tangible activity, on institutions that can create jobs, boost job skills and income from work, steward community resources, and meet basic needs.

Although attention is directed to institutions that operate at the level of the community, many of these institutions have state, regional, or national corollaries. Nonprofit corporations operate at all levels. Community land trusts share characteristics with the Nature Conservancy and similar national organizations. Community development corporations are in many ways like regional power commissions and development agencies such as the Port Authority of New York and New Jersey. Consumer cooperatives have distant connections to national producers' cooperatives marketing agricultural products. These larger institutional examples have both advantages and shortcomings. To the extent that they bring more social surplus under democratic control, they recommend themselves. Our concern here lies with building socially controlled assets at the community level. Discussion proceeds from the broad institutional forms of nonprofit corporations and community development corporations to the more institutionally specific land trusts and workers' and consumers' cooperatives.

Nonprofit Corporations

Nonprofit corporations were introduced in Chapter 3 in the form of philanthropies and foundations, but they operate within a much broader range of activities than handing out money. Groups using this legal organization include clubs and service organizations, hospitals and daycare centers, and medical research and consumer information agencies. One measure of their significance in the U.S. economy is the estimate that between 4 and 5 percent of national income originates in the nonprofit sector.[1]

Nonprofit corporations are the third major institutional form in the United States, after private, for-profit corporations and governmental institutions. They differ from their for-profit counterparts in the restrictions placed on distribution of accrued operating surplus to anyone associated with them. Rather than distributing any surplus they may acquire to their officers or managers, nonprofits can either retain it for future operations or they must give it to other nonprofit organizations.

Section 501(c)3 of the U.S. Internal Revenue Service Code spells out the special status of tax-exempt, nonprofit corporations. This form of nonprofit corporation accounts for approximately a third of all nonprofits. Not only is their income exempt from taxation, but donations to these organizations are deductible from the taxable income of the donor. Nonprofit, tax-exempt organizations are also often exempt from property taxes at the local level, although they may pay a fee in lieu of taxes to help fund services received from local governments. Some of their other benefits include low-cost mailing privileges and exemption from paying Social Security and unemployment taxes unless they choose to do so. They also face some restrictions, such as prohibition from a range of political activities and lobbying.[2]

The nonprofit sector meets an array of needs and demands that people choose to address collectively rather than individually. If a

[1] Weisbrod, *The Nonprofit Sector,* table A.5, p. 172.

[2] Ibid., table A.1, p. 169. See Chapter 3 for discussion of a donor's income tax deduction. Weisbrod, pp. 118–29, reviews these characteristics in discussing whether nonprofit corporations have an advantage in competing with proprietary corporations.

large percentage of the population agrees to meet a need or want, government provision is the probable outcome. Where wants or needs are more diverse, or where smaller numbers of people feel strongly about the desirability of collective action, the nonprofit corporation is a usual organizational vehicle. In some communities, it provides an important vehicle for combining federal, state, and local public funds and private donations for delivery of social services.[3] Two other factors play a part in this choice. One is that a sufficiently strong level of common concern may be difficult to achieve at the national or state level. At the local level shared demographic, cultural, ethnic, and religious or economic status provide a basis for joint action. Although some nonprofit corporations work nationally on a particular problem or goal, many others are products of a critical mass of common need or interest at the local level.

A second factor is the diversity of the population of the United States. The argument that reaching consensus on government delivery of collective goods is less likely here than in countries with more homogeneous populations is often framed in terms of culture and religion, with little attention given to economics. Greater disparity of income, wealth, and life opportunities results from extensive use of markets in the United States. Disparities in access to education, health-care, housing, and other basic needs of life limit the possibility of winning the majority agreements necessary to take collective action.[4] The disparate outcomes intrinsic to market economies reinforce the difficulty of choosing nonmarket alternatives.

No mandate stipulates that nonprofit corporations be structured to function democratically. Communities may find it advantageous to construct boards of directors that are representative of the corporation's constituency, but many do not. The diversity of governance structures within religious organizations, nonprofit hospitals, and national charitable organizations is substantial. Decision-making processes and the ways in which boards of directors are assembled also differ dramatically. Some organizations use open nominating and election procedures, and in others officers are self-perpetuating. Boards

[3] We are indebted to Michael Rotkin for pointing out to us that in Santa Cruz, California, this use of nonprofit organizations has achieved significant results in delivering locally controlled and effective social services.

[4] Other aspects of life count as well. The ideologies of self-reliance and individualism play a reinforcing role. The market's readiness to respond to the demands of those with spending power means that the relatively well-off will tend to find it satisfies their wants and needs.

of directors may have clear roles in setting policy and overseeing the management of an organization, or they may be figurehead or rubber stamp fixtures.

We have chosen two organizations to profile as nonprofit corporations, one urban, the other rural. Each addresses basic human needs at the community level. Each functions as an alternative institution of accumulation and fosters additional development in its community.

Greater Southeast Healthcare System

The Greater Southeast Community Hospital opened in 1966 as a 450-bed hospital in the Anacostia section of Washington, D.C. At that time urban renewal programs displaced many of Washington's poor into the southeast quadrant, while better-off residents left for the suburbs. By the mid-1980s Greater Southeast was surrounded by decaying, poorly serviced neighborhoods, empty storefronts, and a large percentage of residents without health insurance. Moving the hospital to Prince George's County, Maryland, its more affluent suburban service area, seemed a likely option, but instead Greater Southeast took on the task of changing its community.

To serve as a local catalyst for change, Greater Southeast had itself to be healthy.[5] While acute-care occupancy rates declined throughout the country and general hospitals closed, Greater Southeast used astute management and competitive pricing in an expensive urban healthcare market to maintain high occupancy rates. Even though almost one-third of its patients were Medicaid or charity cases, it remained financially sound.

In the 1980s Greater Southeast became the Greater Southeast Healthcare System. Nonprofit subsidiaries were created with community-based boards to pursue new ventures, and activities were organized around a "continuum of healthcare" strategy. The results: "a 180-bed nursing home; a senior daycare center; three ambulatory care and surgicenters in suburban locations; three ethical pharmacies; the first preferred provider organization (PPO) in the region; a durable medical equipment and supply firm; two home health agencies; and

[5] Summary of Greater Southeast's history and activities is based on Barry A. Passett and Jack O. Lanier, "Beyond Health Care: For Greater Southeast, Services Also Focus on Community Development," Greater Southeast Healthcare System, photocopy (Washington, D.C., n.d.), and interview with Barry A. Passett, Washington, D.C., March 23, 1988.

management contracts at a 162-bed nursing home and at a senior daycare center."[6]

Health-related services to the area improved, but neighborhoods in the vicinity of the hospital were still in bad shape; public agency housing had deteriorated, and private owners had little incentive to improve their property. Greater Southeast adopted expanded goals of job creation, housing rehabilitation, and improved public health and education in Anacostia. Its aims were not strictly altruistic; by improving the service area it could attract more privately insured patients and help assure its own sound financial foundation.

Social and public sector entrepreneurship is reflected in Greater Southeast's action:[7] It has tackled three housing projects. In one, it entered into a limited partnership with a local developer to renovate a 160-unit apartment complex. Some units will be used for daycare and other community activities. Renovation of a 275-unit complex within a mile of the hospital is a joint venture between the hospital, the D.C. Department of Housing and Community Development, the Washington Urban League, local developers and banks, and a tenants' organization that will run the complex. A local Baptist church is sponsoring and Greater Southeast's Center for the Aging will manage the third project, housing for low-income elderly tenants. Planning is underway for development of a medical mall and retail space in vacant land on the hospital's campus. The aim is actively to generate growth and attract new businesses to this urban location.

Greater Southeast has sponsored community outreach programs in conjunction with area churches. Many of its neighborhoods have stable populations, and its blood pressure and mobile, low-cost cancer screening programs are important elements of prevention and early warning for residents' healthcare.

This medical complex has also been one of the early bases of an innovative community service bartering system called the Service Credit Volunteer System.[8] Designed to ease problems in the lives of

[6] Passett and Lanier, "Beyond Health Care," p. 4.

[7] Another example of a hospital's strong commitment to remain in and help develop a poor urban neighborhood is Lutheran Medical Center (LMC) in Brooklyn, New York. Barry Passett, Greater Southeast's president, credits George Adams of LMC as the innovator of this process. See Ruth Mintz, "First McGaw Prize Awarded to Lutheran Medical Center," *Metropolitan Hospital* (Fall 1986), 1 and 2; and Mary A. Greyson, "Innovators and Entrepreneurs: 1989," *Hospitals*, May 20, 1989, for a profile of George Adams.

[8] Kathleen Teltech, "Program Allows Elderly to Barter for Services," *New York Times*, February 23, 1987.

elderly residents, participants "bank" hours of service and then use credits for services they need. A small staff matches requests and volunteers and maintains computer records of "accounts." Participants exchange services such as household and yard chores, driving, shopping, and meal preparation. Anacostia's is one of the country's pilot programs, supported by the city council of the District of Columbia and linked to a consortium of fourteen area churches. The program has been funded by grants from the Robert Wood Johnson and Meyer foundations, with seed money from Greater Southeast.

Barry Passett, President of Greater Southeast Community Hospital Foundation and sparkplug for many of these developments, understands the importance of local control of a community's hospital. In a letter to the *New York Times* written in response to articles on the take-over of public hospitals by proprietary, for-profit chains, he emphasized the importance of community control. Proprietary takeovers shut out local businesses and local lenders. Passett made the point that a hospital "is often the biggest business in a community. When a chain takes over, it is not just the profits that flow back to headquarters in Nashville or Beverly Hills. Control of hiring, purchasing of supplies and equipment, banking, insurance, and professional services move there, too." Economics is at issue, but so is power and control.[9]

Although nonprofit hospitals running for-profit subsidiaries are not unusual, Greater Southeast does so as part of a community development strategy. Rush-Presbyterian-St. Luke's Medical Center in Chicago operates Arcventures, Inc., which does business in mail-order drugs, bill collection for physicians and hospitals, home healthcare and "wellness" programs. Profits from Arcventures help to cover losses in other areas of the hospital's operation, such as its health maintenance organization (HMO). Johns Hopkins University and its health system in Baltimore operate the Dome Corporation, a for-profit building renovation firm, developer, office-cleaning and parking-lot management firm. Profits will help establish a "seed fund" to enable the university to commercialize more advantageously technological discoveries.[10] Much of this activity can be seen as institution building that would be hard to distinguish from the goals and methods

[9] Barry A. Passett, *New York Times*, February 19, 1985, letters column.

[10] Milt Freudenheim, "Hospital Ventures: Some Successes," *New York Times*, August 23, 1988.

of conventional business. Indeed, that is part of their appeal to their participants. Greater Southeast has more directly linked its subsidiary ventures to the needs of a community that would have been abandoned by most for-profit ventures. It has structured its operations with boards representing a mix of community constituencies, and is clear about its local redevelopment objectives and the importance of local control.

The Military Highway Water Supply Corporation

Nonprofit corporations are often organized on a shoestring in order to meet basic needs. Few examples could better reflect those conditions than the Military Highway Water Supply Corporation in Progreso, Texas. The nonprofit, tax-exempt corporation supplies water to a group of colonias, small rural clusters of homes, in the Rio Grande Valley of South Texas.[11]

Most of the population of Texas's Hidalgo and Cameron counties is Mexican-American. Although many are among the working poor, some of them have achieved one part of the American dream: home ownership. Colonia residents are estimated to number 200,000 across the border counties of California, Arizona, New Mexico, and Texas. Unfortunately their homes are often situated in unincorporated, unregulated areas where developers are able to sell either lots or completed homes without any water and sewer facilities. As a consequence conditions verging on the kind found in Latin American city-edge colonias (neighborhoods) exist above the Rio Grande.

The South Texas portion of the Rio Grande Valley is home to some of the worst of these conditions because many of its rural unincorporated communities are in areas with high water tables. Lacking sewage handling facilities, they rely on outhouses. Contamination from them, as well as from agricultural chemicals, turns untreated groundwater into a health hazard.

Almost twenty years ago, colonia residents west of Brownsville began work on a solution to their water problem. Led by Arturo Ramirez, they decided that a nonprofit corporation was their best hope. With initial assistance from the Campaign for Human Development, they began with hand-dug wells, improved drainage ditches, and a tighter watch over the disposition of pesticides. Gradually they

[11] Summary is from interview with Adan Cantu, manager, and Damasio Cano, assistant manager, Military Highway Water Supply Corporation, Progreso, Texas, June 8, 1987.

tapped the Farmers Home Administration, Economic Development Administration, Texas Department of Community Affairs, and other federal and state agencies for the funds to capitalize purification facilities, pumping stations, and pipelines. The corporation's first employees were paid with Comprehensive Employment Training Act funds. Customers were recruited at area churches. They paid a $50 membership fee, a small deposit, and the cost of connecting their plumbing to the company's lines. Then many installed their first indoor plumbing.

The corporation began operating its own treatment plant in 1976. Today it employs eleven and serves nearly six thousand residential, farm, and commercial customers. Part of its expansion came from buying out a failing private water supply system that was in trouble with the health department. The buyout included crucial additional rights to draw water from the Rio Grande.

The Military Highway Water Supply Corporation cannot tax the residents of its service area to cover costs; it struggles to collect the $6 to $10 per month fee per household. The $1.5 million per year in sales covers most costs, including maintenance of the system and some reserves for new equipment. Still, outside grants subsidize expansion to more isolated communities that would otherwise go without water. Grants have also helped planning for waste-water (sewage) collection and treatment.

Progreso's water system is a model of community self-help.[12] Indeed, visitors from India and Pakistan, Africa, the Philippines, and Mexico have traveled to this Texas crossroads to understand better how such a poor area of scattered housing clusters met one of its most basic needs. Nearly $8 million in assets that accumulated through delivery of water and energetic pursuit of funding from governmental and philanthropic repositories of social surplus have made the area a better and safer place in which to live. The accumulated assets and cash flow of this nonprofit organization provide a basis, meager but tangible, for further expansion of services unavailable through public action.

[12] This project also illustrates one of the fundamental problems of self-help strategies for development. The energy and resources used to create this water supply system could have been used to begin the battle for closer regulation of developers or for more customary public water supply (which could have led to better regulation of developers) many years ago. Lack of political power among colonia residents made those alternatives seem very hard to win.

A more universal form of help may finally be on the way for many colonia residents. Their squalid conditions and related health problems are no longer being ignored by county, state, and federal officials.[13] In Texas, much of the credit for this change belongs to two member organizations of the Texas Industrial Areas Foundation. Valley Interfaith in the Rio Grande Valley and the El Paso Interreligious Sponsoring Organization (EPISO) in the northwestern corner of the state have been fighting for public action on residents' water and sewer needs for approximately five years. Rather than continuing to pass the buck to federal or county government, the State of Texas is pursuing funding to build water and sewer plants to serve the colonias. Residents will pay fees for services just as they do in thousands of other American cities and communities. Federal action is also being considered as part of a package of legislation dealing with the U.S.-Mexican border area.

Nonprofit corporations deliver essential services, create jobs, and function as institutions of accumulation within communities. They are more likely than proprietary organizations to be locally controlled, and to have boards of directors that represent a broad range of the community's population. As alternative institutions of accumulation they are not channeling social surplus to distant shareholders. Each of these attributes can have positive implications for community development.

Community Development Corporations

Community development corporations (CDCs) had their start in the late 1960s. Promoted by the federal Office of Economic Opportunity and Ford Foundation, these nonprofit, community-based organizations were intended to stimulate both economic and political development. As sponsoring organizations, they were to receive and disperse federal and foundation funds to initiate local development projects such as job training and small business development. They were also to be locally accountable and democratically controlled, thus providing experience in progressive local governance for community residents. Guidelines for their operation were broad, and their

[13] Peter Applebone, "At Texas Border, Hopes for Sewers and Water," *New York Times*, January 3, 1989.

results mixed. One early evaluation found positive correlation between degree of community representation on boards of directors and staffs and their economic achievements. Later in the 1970s a critical study argued that CDCs simply set up a new governing apparatus in poor urban neighborhoods and that they were not very responsive to community needs.[14]

By the end of their first decade of operation, the rules of the game for CDCs had been extensively revised. Federal funding through the Community Services Administration (CSA) was scaled back, and eventually the Reagan administration abolished the office. CDCs had to be much more self-sufficient economically. Organizations that had the potential to address issues of power and economics within poor urban neighborhoods became, through the late Carter and Reagan years, involved with entrepreneurial ventures.[15] If power was addressed at all for poor and often minority areas, it would be through the traditional path of business development. Multifaceted but difficult to measure objectives of the early years gave way to the easier-to-measure but limited goal of revenue to maintain operations.

Ghettos exist because resources and income are largely absent. CDCs face these unlikely conditions under which to establish successful business ventures. In most CDCs, a nonprofit parent organization with a broad social and economic development mandate operates for-profit subsidiaries.

Mexican American Unity Council

San Antonio, Texas, has long wrestled with issues of growth and development and with the distribution of the resultant benefits and costs. Since 1974 it has been home to Communities Organized for Public Service (COPS), well known for its work to win basic services for the city's poorer neighborhoods and residents. San Antonio is also home to another organization that works for the improvement of life for the city's poor, Mexican-American population. The Mexican

[14] Jerry Cromwell and Peter Merrill, "Minority Business Performance and the Community Development Corporation," *Review of Black Political Economy* 3:3 (1973), 65–81; Harry E. Berndt, *New Rulers in the Ghetto: The CDC and Urban Poverty* (Westport, Conn., 1977).

[15] For an overview of this phenomenon, and examples from enterprise development in Chicago, see Wim Wiewel and Robert Mier, "Enterprise Activities of Not-for-Profit Organizations: Surviving the New Federalism?" in *Local Economies in Transition: Policy Realities and Development Potentials,* Edward M. Bergman, ed. (Durham, N.C., 1986), pp. 205–25.

American Unity Council, Inc. (MAUC) has attracted and generated resources for its target population since 1967, with the purpose of carrying out "social, physical and economic revitalization" in San Antonio's west and southwest quadrants.[16]

MAUC emphasizes traditional strategies of local economic growth to reach its goals. As a community development corporation it is a nonprofit, tax-exempt organization. However, it has for-profit subsidiaries under a holding company called MAUC Industries, Inc. that serves as a vehicle for financial and real estate development. The MAUC Financial Company includes a minority enterprise small business investment company (MESBIC) that qualifies for low-cost loans to businesses owned by minorities, a small business investment company that can provide debt and equity participation, and a small business management services firm that can assist firms and provide individuals with income tax assistance.

MAUC Industries realty branch does land-use studies, as well as evaluations of properties and acquisition and development. Its Neighborhood Housing Services provides low-cost home improvement loans to low-income households and operates a construction company for residential and commercial building rehabilitation.

Operating divisions within MAUC address often parallel physical and economic community problems and their social, educational, and health-related aspects. Examples on the social front include child and family mental health outreach and clinical services, an alcoholism residential program, and a pre-therapeutic nursery and daycare facility for abused, neglected, or disadvantaged three- to five-year-old children. Projects affecting the economic and physical environment of MAUC's Special Impact Area include a housing project for the elderly of 106 units with a resident support program; the MAUC Center,

[16] See David R. Johnson, John A. Booth, and Richard J. Harris, eds., *The Politics of San Antonio* (Lincoln, Neb., 1983), and David C. Perry, "Sunbelt Boosterism: The Politics of Postwar Growth and Annexation in San Antonio," in *The Rise of Sunbelt Cities,* Perry and Alfred J. Watkins, eds. (Beverly Hills, Calif., 1977), pp. 151–68. COPS and its affiliates have been written about extensively. See Harry C. Boyte, *Community Is Possible: Repairing America's Roots* (New York, 1984), chap. 5; Geoffrey Rips, "A New Spirit Flows along the Rio Grande," *In These Times,* May 18–24, 1988, 12, 13, and 22, and his "Privatization: The Next Big Lucha," *The Texas Observer,* February 21, 1986; and several of the articles in Johnson, Booth, and Harris, eds., *The Politics of San Antonio.* COPS is another member of the Texas Industrial Areas Foundation, introduced earlier in this chapter. Summary is from an interview with Domingo Bueno, President, Mexican American Unity Council, San Antonio, Texas, June 5, 1987; "Overview of the Mexican American Unity Council," MAUC, photocopy (n.d.); and the Mexican American Unity Council, *1986 Annual Report.*

formerly a run-down and unused elementary school that now houses MAUC's offices and community organizations such as Bexar County's Women's Center and a branch of the San Antonio Public Library; and rehabilitation of housing for low-income residents.

In recent years MAUC has become entrepreneurial in a more traditional way. It has entered into partnerships with private developers on a six hundred–room downtown Hyatt hotel and a smaller motor hotel adjacent to its apartments for the elderly. The equity position it holds in the Hyatt has been used to assure access to contracts and jobs there for minority-owned firms and minority residents. Major new projects include participation in a large medical office complex that will house daycare facilities and a grocery store and in a new industrial park intended to attract jobs. The ninety-five–acre industrial park, including light industry, offices, and retail space, is a joint venture with the East Los Angeles Community Union, the country's largest CDC. The City of San Antonio granted a loan of $700,000 for the park with the help of COPS. Funds will be repaid to a revolving loan fund for community development.

Entrepreneurial activity has also included losses and setbacks. Reconstruction of an urban grocery store proved to be a venture that failed. When land originally acquired for the industrial park was affected by local U.S. Air Force operations, a new site had to be found, causing a substantial delay in construction.

Private funds for MAUC and other large CDCs have come principally from Ford Foundation. Its contribution accounted for 22 percent of MAUC's operating budget in 1985–86. Ford assists CDCs with established track records to develop income streams that will sustain them. MAUC and other CDCs are pursuing social surplus more directly than they have before. Rather than receive surplus indirectly from foundation or federal sources, they are appropriating it from ownership positions in the local economy.

Can this form of organization work for the community? Part of the answer is clearly yes, but the best indicators of positive achievements are not captured in the simple measure of profitability. For-profit subsidiaries can be considered successful if they bring new goods or services into the community, or displace higher cost providers, or those that employ fewer local workers or extract rents and profits from the community. Their value will be difficult to measure precisely, because it includes weighing the good done by the social service aspects of the CDC (job training, neighborhood repair, increased access to healthcare) against the costs to those from whom any profit is extracted. Ultimately, profits made by subsidiaries are returned to the community much more surely than if appropriated by business owners who live elsewhere or if paid out to stockholders. Few if any stockholders live in poor neighborhoods.

In our analysis of the economic impact of a McDonald's restaurant on a community, we raised the possibility of a somewhat different outcome if the business was owned by a local nonprofit organization. In their quest for an income stream, community development corporations have been drawn to franchises. They are generally set up as profit-making subsidiaries of the nonprofit CDC, and they provide the opportunity for business to develop with a proven product and operating system, established training program, and corporate assistance in market analysis and business planning. Examples of this trend include Black People's Unity Market (BPUM) in Camden, New Jersey, a for-profit corporation that operates Burger King and Chicken George franchises. West Oak Lane Community Development Corporation in a predominantly African-American inner-city area of Philadelphia owned a subsidiary that operated a Dunkin' Donuts franchise.[17] Despite concern for the food products provided and the typical terms of employment, these franchises provide a business service in their neighborhoods, jobs and job training, and channel any profit they make back into their communities through their parent CDCs. Depending on local purchase arrangements for supplies, rental payments, and other specific conditions of the franchise, they could do far more for their neighborhoods than our corporate-owned McDonald's example would.

What does the for-profit orientation of a CDC's subsidiaries do to its operation? Although the answer is not yet certain, emerging patterns cause concern. For-profit activity tends to be carried out privately, increasing tension within CDCs. The parent organization attempts to maintain a broadly representative and democratic board that is charged with overseeing its for-profit subsidiaries, yet it is financially dependent on them and must allow them to operate relatively independently. Tensions gradually erode the community-

[17] We are indebted to Michael Freedland of the Corporation for Enterprise Development, Washington, D.C., for bringing this trend to our attention. See Robert E. Barragan and Michael Freedland, "Restaurant Franchises: Another CED Strategy," *Economic Development and Law Center Report* 16 (Fall 1986), 1–11.

based, open, and responsive side of CDC operations. In sum, the potential of CDCs as agencies of political and social empowerment seems to have diminished in the 1980s. At the same time, their role as agents of economic development has been more narrowly defined into traditional business practice. Yes, CDCs provide development potential, but it is safely mainstream. CDCs may end up providing apprenticeships for members of chambers of commerce.

Another important shift is embodied in the changing nature of CDCs. In their early form they served a redistributive function, at least partly channeling national resources into areas that needed development, where people were organized to help bring it about. Language that refers to "mature" CDCs being "weaned" glosses over the question of whether those same areas should be told to find internally the resources they need. Development requires social surplus. The for-profit activity of CDCs can substitute for profit extraction by other privately owned operations, but by definition the surplus available for appropriation, by CDCs or private corporations from outside the community, is limited.

Community Land Trusts

Community land trusts are another example of a specialized organization that uses the legal form of nonprofit corporation. These trusts cause changes in the normal pattern of property rights and in market determination of access and price of the commodities land and housing. They provide a means of holding legal title and rights to property in a social, rather than individual or business-directed, corporate form. The nonprofit corporation holds property in trust, supervises it, and maintains it as an asset. Most have open memberships and an elected board of directors that includes users of the land and other interested residents of the community. Their life spans are meant to exceed that of any of their members. Bylaws spell out democratic practices.

Early interest in trusts had vague roots in back-to-the-land trends of the late 1960s and early 1970s and in the rediscovered Native Americans' concept of stewardship of the land. The thinking of Henry George and Mahatma Gandhi have also influenced their development. Today they have taken concrete form in trusts to encourage affordable housing and in trusts to preserve open land. Greenspace is being protected in some parts of the country by formation of trusts that are funded, in part at least, by a voluntary local "green tax," paid by consumers of certain products.[18]

The 1980s have seen increasing public awareness of America's housing problems. Homeless people are the visible extreme of conditions that include a diminished federal commitment to build housing, rapid escalation in housing prices which excludes a larger percentage of people from the possibility of home acquisition, and rents rising faster than incomes. The country's working poor are often challenged to pay rent that can require from a third to half of their take-home pay. These conditions have had an impact on land trusts.[19] The trusts provide one means of developing a sector of socially owned housing resources, an alternative that can coexist with privately owned and public housing.

Community land trusts have been formed by churches, community organizations, and low-income people themselves. They are designed to take land out of the speculative realm; many restrict the exchange of housing located on their land in ways that limit its price escalation. Typically land trusts in urban areas will buy housing that comes on the market, place the land in the trust, and renovate and sell the housing to low- or moderate-income households. Households that cannot afford a down payment may get help through low-cost loans from a city housing department, or the trust may allow some or all rental payments to count toward a down payment. Since housing is sold without the land it rests on, and because renovations are often done by nonprofit organizations that use voluntary labor, housing prices are kept below those in the surrounding market. The contractual agreement with the trust generally limits the benefit of future appreciation in price for the owner to what has been paid plus some stipulated measure that accounts for inflation; the housing has to be resold to the trust, and the trust will again sell it under its special

[18] An example is the Finger Lakes Green Fund, based in Ithaca, New York. In addition to establishing trusts, it aims to restore the environment and educate for environmental protection.

[19] In terms of housing, community land trusts are one small element of a solution to a massive problem. On the scope of the problem, see Rachel G. Bratt, Chester Hartman, and Ann Meyerson, eds., *Critical Perspectives on Housing* (Philadelphia, 1986), part I. For concrete proposals for solutions to problems in housing, see Dick Cluster et al., *The Right to Housing: A Blueprint for Housing the Nation* (Washington, D.C., 1989). Information on community land trusts and their use in solving housing problems can be obtained from the Institute for Community Economics (ICE) (57 School Street, Springfield, MA 01105).

restrictions; and rights of inheritance are preserved. A recent trend is for the land trust to establish housing units as part of a limited equity housing cooperative.[20] As principal users of the land, homeowners make up a majority of the trust's or the co-op's membership, and with other trust members they manage the organization.

For households, land trust housing arrangements and limited equity co-op housing eliminate home ownership as a vehicle of speculation, but not savings. Equity is built in housing, but it is not a means of making consistently substantial gains because of changing market conditions. Advocates of community land trusts argue that they rearrange property rights in a logical way. Escalating home prices reflect changes in the community that should accrue to community-based organizations, rather than to individual owners, developers, or speculators. Most important, land trust–based housing can remain affordable. It is isolated from market conditions that might otherwise put it out of reach of a substantial portion of community residents.

Successful land trusts are operating in communities as diverse as a nine-town area in New Hampshire (the Franklin Area Community Land Trust) and a low-income section of Dallas, Texas (Common Ground Economic Development Corporation). The South Atlanta Land Trust (SALT) expands and maintains a stock of affordable housing, but also blocks clearance of much of the area's older housing stock to make room for commercial development pushing out from the city's center. It refurbishes housing, brokers mortgages for their buyers, and holds the land under them in trust. The Community Land Trust in Burlington, Vermont, was assisted by a $200,000 appropriation of seed money from Community Development Block Grant funds by the city government, and some of its housing has been renovated by the Burlington Youth Employment Program.[21] These examples and most other urban land trusts are involved in both single and multi-unit housing.

Land trusts can marshal resources from volunteers, future home occupants, community groups, commercial lenders, local business donors, and city governments to address the pressing local problem of housing. In conjunction with limited equity housing cooperatives and municipal and mutual housing, community land trusts provide an

[20] See *Community Economics* 18 (Summer 1989), and subsequent issues.

[21] Bill Dedman, "Anybody Can Sit out There and Mouth Off—He Gets Things Done," *The Atlanta Constitution,* May 4, 1988. Summary is from multiple issues of *Community Economics.*

avenue to housing assets that are held in the community, and controlled by it. When they are created to preserve open land, they do so for public use, even though the land will be maintained by a community-based, nongovernmental organization.

Pension Funds and Union Trust Funds

States and cities are eyeing their employees' pension funds as a source of cash for rebuilding infrastructure and undertaking other expensive projects. Managers of the funds face the task of dealing with the pressure imposed on them to use these large pools of invested funds for more "socially conscious" projects, but at the same time fulfilling their legal obligation to run portfolios in the best interest of their members. That has generally meant seeking the highest possible return within the moderate risk profile deemed suitable for this form of investment. Public employee pension funds are especially vulnerable to pressure because their managers are often appointed by governors and mayors. Pension funds of private employers are less vulnerable; the chance is far less that social obligations would be added to their responsibility to maximize returns.

Pension fund resources are of such large magnitude that, like the growing surplus in the Social Security trust fund, they draw attention and debate over their use. State and union pension funds are invested in public projects mostly through bondholding. The Council of Institutional Investors, representing sixty union and state pension funds worth approximately $300 billion, seeks clearer guidelines to protect its fund managers from undue pressure to underwrite the specific pet projects of any appointed or elected official.[22] Yet those interested in local initiatives will continue to search for ways in which these funds can be targeted to social projects such as low-cost housing, rather than simply being invested in an undifferentiated mix of whatever Wall Street has to offer.

[22] See the sweeping proposals for redirecting use of pension funds in Carnoy and Shearer, *Economic Democracy*, pp. 96–123; Sarah Bartlett, "Pension Fund Strategy Shift Is Assailed," *New York Times*, December 5, 1989. A summary of American Federation of Labor–Congress of Industrial Organizations (AFL-CIO) proposals for pension fund reform and a review of alternative governance systems used for pension programs can be found in Teresa Ghilarducci, "Strategic Uses of Pension Funds since 1978," *Review of Radical Political Economics* 20:4 (1988), 23–39.

Public regulation blocks direct, democratic control by employees over their own pension funds.[23] Some fund assets, however, can be used innovatively at the local level. Teamster pension fund ownership of land made the union a natural partner in the Santa Cruz development of housing for the elderly described in Chapter 3. In Boston the highly publicized development of low-cost housing by the Bricklayers and Masons Union used pension-fund money. The bank's $1.2 million loan for the project was made at a below-market interest rate because the pension fund's certificate of deposit served as a compensating balance.[24] For one of its two housing developments, the union's nonprofit housing corporation received city land from an abandoned Boston school for one dollar. Thomas McIntyre, union vice president, acted as contractor while paid by the union. Bricklayers and other Boston area union members worked in both projects, at union scale of course.

Pension funds are built from contributions of employers as part of their compensation to their workers. They are a form of enforced saving, administered by trustees, that will be made available to sustain people during retirement. Strictly speaking, they are a necessary labor cost because they help maintain the labor force. Yet as pools of savings, they are invested, and they gain income from social surplus. Those in the public sector or under union control are more likely to be drawn into innovative, public, and third sector forms of investment.

An innovative union trust fund resulted from bargaining by Local 26 of the Hotel and Restaurant Employees International Union, which largely represents women and minority members engaged in service work in Boston hotels. Boston's fast rising housing costs through the 1980s had made affordable, decent housing for wage earners scarce. The union bargained for a trust fund to help its members gain housing. The fund will grow from a five-cent-per-hour contribution by employers, which will generate an estimated one-third of a million dollars per year.[25] The fund will be available to union members for down payments on homes or for the initial contracting costs for rentals.

[23] Carnoy and Shearer, *Economic Democracy*, pp. 102–12.

[24] Paul Goldberger, "High Marks for Low-Cost Housing in Boston," *New York Times*, November 6, 1988; Barry Shlachter, "Beantown's Robin Hood Offers Inexpensive Homes," *Ithaca Journal*, August 28, 1986.

[25] Mark Feinberg, "Affordable Housing for the Union," *In These Times*, February 22–March 1, 1989, p. 5; Hotel and Restaurant Employees International Union, Local 26, news release of December 18, 1989.

The fund will be used for loans, long-term forgivable loans, and grants depending on members' income-based levels of need. It will also be used to provide collateral for member participation in city, state, and private-sector housing programs.

Implementation of this trust depends on a change in the federal Taft-Hartley Act, which precludes housing trusts from union trust funds. That change makes employers nervous because unions will be debating whether this is a worthwhile area for bargaining. To the extent that they can make new net gains in compensation through trusts of this kind for their members, unions will squeeze their employers' claim on surplus.

Consumers' and Workers' Cooperatives

Despite the fact that cooperatives have been in relative eclipse over the past decade, they remain one of the first institutional forms that people turn to for alternatives to mainstream organizations. From our perspective, their appeal lies in the fact that they are typically more democratic institutions than profit-making corporations, that in general they are locally based, and that, overcoming some difficulties, they can be effective institutions of accumulation. We will expand on each of these points after briefly distinguishing two forms of co-ops.[26]

Consumers' cooperatives are located in communities across the country. They range in size from neighborhood natural food stores to the giant Greenbelt Co-op in suburban Washington, D.C., and Recreational Equipment Incorporated (REI) based in Seattle, Washington. They provide high quality consumer goods and services to their members at a reasonable price. One form that consumers' co-ops can take is limited equity housing co-ops, mentioned earlier in this chapter. Small consumers' co-ops, especially those dealing in food, tend to use volunteer labor from their members. On the other hand, some larger food operations, such as Puget Consumer Co-op in Seattle, have a unionized workforce that plays a role, with consumer-

[26] In principle, producers' co-ops that are active in processing and marketing agricultural products could be included in this discussion. They could help keep value added in the community, and they too can be controlled democratically by their members. In practice, most with which we are familiar serve a wide geographical area and operate more like traditional businesses than democratic organizations.

directors, in running the cooperative. Their volunteer labor is confined to membership development and consumer education.

Workers' cooperatives use co-op principles to structure a producers' rather than a consumers' organization. The workers of the firm are its "patrons." They choose a board of directors, make policy decisions, and hire and fire managers just as members of other cooperatives do. Rather than capital hiring labor, as in the conventional firm, workers "hire" capital. They use their own and borrowed funds to capitalize their business and then run it as equals. Workers' co-ops have existed for over a century in this country. They are far fewer in number than consumers' co-ops. The one industry in which they have maintained a long-term and substantial presence is plywood manufacturing, where cooperative mills have for decades accounted for 10 to 15 percent of the nation's production of softwood plywood.[27]

Most co-ops reflect the Rochdale principles, rules of operation devised by consumers' co-op pioneers in England in the mid-nineteenth century. The Rochdale principles specified that cooperatives would operate on the basis of one person, one vote. For-profit corporations allocate a vote to each share of outstanding common stock; one's financial stake in the firm determines one's voting power. Those with no shares, or no money to buy stock, have no voice in decision making. Co-ops specify equality of voting power among all who participate in them. Consumers' co-ops generally have a nominal membership fee (REI's is $10 for a lifetime), and membership is open to all. Members divide surplus accumulated at the end of an accounting period on the basis of their patronage (usage) of the co-op. Workers' cooperatives have restricted membership and sometimes hybrid stock ownership stipulations, but members are allotted only one vote no matter what their level of lending or investment in the firm, their years of seniority, or their job description. In both kinds of co-ops, organizational control and control over surplus rests with members alone. They typically elect a rotating board of directors, and the board sets policy, works with people in management positions, and monitors day-to-day operations. Since all income after expenses and taxes belongs to worker-members, and the right to participate in decision

[27] For an overview of this history, see Derek C. Jones, "American Producer Cooperatives and Employee-Owned Firms: A Historical Perspective," in *Worker Cooperatives in America*, Robert Jackall and Henry M. Levin, eds. (Berkeley, Calif., 1984), pp. 37–56. See Christopher E. Gunn, *Workers' Self-Management in the United States* (Ithaca, 1984), chap. 4, for a discussion of plywood manufacturing cooperatives.

making derives from work, not ownership, outsiders have no economic incentive to hold stock in co-ops.

Both workers' and consumers' co-ops are usually locally based organizations. Workers' co-ops generally number no more than several hundred members, working at one location. Consumers' co-ops serve those who can get to the store, live in the housing, or visit the clinic. (REI is an exception; it built a national mail-order business before expanding retail outlets into ten other states.) Most co-ops have defined local regions of operation, but many reach well beyond their local environment for the products they sell or incorporate into their manufactured products. Their own operations, however—the income they generate, members they serve, and accumulation they create—tend to be geographically defined.

Given the conditions discussed above, cooperatives would seem to be ideal alternative institutions of accumulation. However, historical evidence and some basic theory indicate problems in this regard. Most co-ops have been formed by people of moderate financial means. Consumers' co-ops have often grown out of neighborhood food-buying clubs, where voluntary work and distribution through private homes and transportation have helped keep the cost of food to a minimum. This low-cost philosophy has carried over to the co-ops. Initial capitalization of space and equipment often came from loans by co-op members. Once in operation, the co-ops struggled to make new investment in physical assets; modern facilities and labor-saving equipment were not only costly, but suspect in some circles as well. In sum, most consumers' co-ops have had difficulty in building reserves to assure smooth long-term operation, much less funds to launch additional activities.

The consumers' cooperative we profile here is a large and sophisticated example of the breed. Its technological and knowledge-based services and its size preclude the more direct control that numerous local co-ops provide to their members, but this form of organization clearly is not limited in application to small local suppliers of goods and services.

Group Health Cooperative

Group Health Cooperative (GHC) of Puget Sound is the product of a sustained effort to develop consumer-controlled provision of healthcare in Seattle. Its inspiration came from a combination of industrial prepaid contract medicine practiced in the Pacific Northwest since the 1920s, and the first medical cooperative in the United States, founded in Elk City, Oklahoma, in 1928. The King County Medical Society, the Seattle-area American Medical Association affiliate, fought the co-op throughout its early years. It barred GHC's physicians from specialty certification—and even from the privilege of admitting patients—at other area hospitals. In 1951 the Washington State Supreme Court found the medical society acting in restraint of trade, and Group Health Cooperative had established legal precedent against medical society resistance to group practices.[28]

Today GHC is the largest health maintenance organization (HMO) in the Northwest and the tenth largest HMO in the country.[29] It is also a cooperative, nonprofit organization governed by a consumer-elected, eleven-member board of trustees. The co-op expanded across Washington and into western Idaho with the acquisition of Group Health Northwest in Spokane. Its enrollment is over 430,000 healthcare consumers, and its revenues in 1989 exceeded $450 million. GHC is Washington state's ninth largest employer, and it provides medical care to one of every eleven of the state's residents. Approximately 80 percent of the co-op's enrollees are members of group healthcare plans, funded in whole or part by over three thousand employers.

GHC's board contracts with its medical staff for services to enrollees. Elected consumers make up a majority of the members of three regional councils, twenty-one medical center councils, and its council assembly, all of which monitor delivery of care and advise the board of trustees. Special interest caucuses operate on women's, mental health, and senior healthcare issues. Mail referendums and annual meetings are used to shape policy advice.[30]

Seattle is often described as a "middle-class" city. Its resident base certainly includes both employed and unemployed poor and homeless, but decades of industrial employment supplemented in recent years by an expanding service sector have diminished poverty there compared to many other U.S. cities. GHC membership consists of an

[28] Group Health Care of Puget Sound, *History* (Seattle, Wash., n.d.).

[29] Health maintenance organizations are paid a fixed fee for each of their members. The fee covers the care needs of the member, no matter how much or little care is required in the period covered by the fee. Employers often pay the fee as a fringe benefit to a wage or salary, much as they pay for an employee's health insurance. The largest and best known HMO in the country is Kaiser, which has six million members.

[30] Group Health Care of Puget Sound, *Fact Sheet* (Seattle, Wash., February 1989), p. 1, and 1990 update.

employed and well-educated segment of the general population, which provides an advantageous group of clients for healthcare, and the co-op works to enhance their well-being: screening programs for breast, cervical, and prostate cancer; alcoholism and obesity treatment; promotion of bicycle safety helmets; and programs to assist members to stop smoking. GHC has been a strong supporter of Washington's Basic Health Plan, one of the first state efforts to provide health insurance for all citizens; it provides care to Basic Health Plan participants on a break-even basis.[31]

Despite substantial increases in expenses in the mid-1980s, Group Health Cooperative's annual per capita healthcare delivery costs were approximately 20 percent below the national average in 1987. That meant lower costs to employers who paid HMO fees and to consumers when they paid all or part of the fees directly. The annual revenues to this system, now close to half a billion dollars, remain and recirculate in the state more than they might with other providers. The GHC *1988 Annual Report* states that ninety-nine cents of each dollar of revenue were used for members' healthcare but advises that more than one percent of the co-op's revenues be placed in reserve for new construction and renewal of existing facilities and equipment.[32] The struggle to maintain reinvestment is a common one for cooperatives, but the other outstanding feature of this operation is that profits are not wrung from the provision of healthcare to send to wealthy stockholders. This advantage, in addition to consumer and local control, makes GHC an attractive alternative to proprietary hospitals and industry-dominated insurers.

Workers' co-ops have also wrestled with their own versions of economic pressures that curtailed their ability to accumulate. One was a historical tendency to underinvest because of inefficient financing mechanisms and structures. In numerous American cases, workers' co-ops gained their equity capital from members. No provisions were made to return invested capital to departing or retiring members or to pay for its use while it was invested. Thus, only under unusual circumstances would members be inclined to invest substantial amounts—and to continue investing—in their firms. Compounding the problem was the economic objective of most members of a

[31] Group Health Care of Puget Sound, *1988 Annual Report* (Seattle, Wash.), p. 5.

[32] Ibid., pp. 14, 4.

workers' co-op to maximize their current income, even though new investment could help assure higher future incomes. These forces combined to make accumulation, even for normal business operations, a challenge. Theoretical advances and growing awareness of the dramatic success of the Spanish co-ops of Mondragon occurred in the 1970s; both point to solutions to the accumulation problem. They include recoverable equity commitments, payment of interest for the use of members' invested funds, and stipulated percentages of income mandated for reinvestment.[33]

Cooperatives must be successful alternative businesses before they can take on additional burdens of accumulating surplus for other uses. They have to pay living wages and benefits to their workers, satisfy their customers, and carry on sufficient accumulation of operating surplus to assure their own survival and development.

Operating outside the mainstream of American commercial activity, but in competition with it, sheer survival for co-ops can be a tall order. However, co-ops can be alternative institutions of accumulation in at least two important ways. One is inherent when they succeed. Their own growth and development mean that more commercial activity takes place under local, democratic control. Accumulation thus takes place under more progressive conditions than it would if these were capitalist firms.

Second, successful workers' co-ops have the ability to tax themselves in order to contribute to the development of their community. While co-ops pay taxes at the federal, state, and local levels, they can also earmark part of their earnings for projects that they wish to support. In Ithaca, New York, Alternatives Fund, a group based on

[33] For examples of U.S. workers' cooperatives and case studies on their operation, see Jackall and Levin, eds., *Worker Cooperatives in America*, and Gunn, *Workers' Self-Management*. On members' investment see Gunn, pp. 32–51, and appendix 2, pp. 223–34. Important theoretical insight into the historical problems of the financing of workers' co-ops was achieved by Jaroslav Vanek in the early 1970s. Mondragon's successful financial arrangements were devised by its founders and elaborated in a contract of association between member co-ops and the Caja Laboral Popular, Mondragon's credit union-bank discussed in Chapter 3. It stipulates that the co-op maintain interest-bearing individual accounts for members which reflect their mandated initial investment in the co-op, as well as gains and losses from operations. Most of their share of profits (surplus) must stay in the co-op in this account. Members who retire or leave these co-ops must take their accumulated funds with them, and they surrender any further right to participate in the co-op's decision making. Another part of surplus must be allocated to the co-op's collectively held capitalization. See Henk Thomas and Chris Logan, *Mondragon: An Economic Analysis* (Boston, 1982), chap. 6, and Whyte and Whyte, *Making Mondragon*.

this principle, assists co-op business start-ups. It had problems initially because it specified member co-ops' contributions based on sales, which had a very different impact on members operating in different industries with different cost structures. Eventually, member firms negotiated their contributions. Mondragon operates differently, stipulating that 10 percent of annual surplus be devoted to a social fund for community projects.[34] In addition to these prescribed arrangements, individual action on the part of co-ops has made use of their ability to accumulate funds and direct them to development of other "third-sector" organizations. Reforestation co-ops in the Pacific Northwest made direct loans from their reserves to assist the start-up of other co-ops.[35] Some co-ops have deposited their reserve accounts in area credit unions with the stipulation that they be used to make certain types of development loans, or parts of their surplus can be made available to area development loan funds. Both actions assure that lending is done under the supervision of people trained to evaluate the condition of potential borrowers.

Many co-ops in the United States have worked to keep their differences from traditional businesses under wraps. They have operated under the presumption that their cooperative form would make them suspect to customers, suppliers, or the government, and in various ways harm their operations.[36] From our perspective a healthy third sector will encourage co-ops to advertise their differences, and the reasons for them, and to attract business by doing so. Some co-ops have engaged in this activity in the past; stronger information-sharing, technical assistance, training and advocacy organizations would enable others to join them.

[34] These funds are administered by each co-op's social council, the organ that sets personnel and worker health and safety policies for Mondragon's co-ops. While conducting interviews at Mondragon, our inquiries as to the uses to which social funds have been put brought answers as diverse as expenditure on health and education in the community, public-building restoration, and even an annual dinner for the families of co-op members. From interviews with staff members of the Caja Laboral Popular, June 27–30, 1988.

[35] See Christopher E. Gunn, "Hoedads Co-op: Democracy and Cooperation at Work," in *Worker Cooperatives in America*, Jackall and Levin, eds., p. 160.

[36] A case in point is the plywood cooperatives. Their names, business letterhead, and advertising give little indication of their co-op status. They argue that this practice helps them avoid various forms of discrimination, as well as what they have argued is harassment by the U.S. Internal Revenue Service. For their history, see Katrina V. Berman, *Worker-Owned Plywood Firms: An Economic Analysis* (Pullman, Wash., 1967). For an indication of their pragmatic approach to business, see Edward S. Greenberg, *Workplace Democracy: The Political Effects of Participation* (Ithaca, 1986).

Work Collectives

Work collectives exist as informal organizations of work that produce or sell goods or services. Some use the legal form of partnerships, and others use cooperative or corporate legal forms. Their work structures and relations among members are often very informal. They may provide principal means of livelihood to their member-workers or give organizational focus to voluntary work. The degree to which they use traditional hierarchy, power-sharing, consensual decision making, or hybrid techniques to get business done varies widely.[37]

An important example of a work collective that has had a major impact on women's healthcare is the Boston Women's Health Book Collective (BWHBC).[38] Royalty income from several publications, most notably *Our Bodies, Ourselves* and *The New Our Bodies, Ourselves*,[39] has provided a stream of funding for a variety of activities: to sustain outreach work through the Collective's Women's Health Information Center; to distribute thousands of free copies of the Spanish-language edition of *Our Bodies, Ourselves* to family planning and community clinics in the United States and Latin America; to help set up Community Works, a Boston-area funding agency for social change organizations as an alternative to the United Way; and to carry out numerous other projects related to women's health issues both in the United States and abroad.

In recent years, annual royalty income of approximately $100,000 has paid BWHBC members and staff for their work and sustained the Women's Health Information Center. Outside foundation funding

[37] For an overview of the incidence and history of recent collectives and cooperatives, see Robert Jackall and Joyce Crain, "The Shape of the Small Worker Cooperative Movement," in *Worker Cooperatives in America*, Jackall and Levin, eds., pp. 88–108. An introduction to organizational aspects of a collective can be found in Barbara Beckwith, "Boston Women's Health Care Collective: Women Empowering Women," *Women & Health* 10:1 (1985), 1–7.

[38] Information on the Boston Women's Health Care Collective is from Barbara Beckwith, ibid.; Judy Norsigian and Wendy Coppedge Sanford, "Ten Years in the 'Our Bodies, Ourselves' Collective," *Women & Therapy* 6:1 and 2 (1987), 287–92; Gene Bruce, "Our Bodies, Growing Older," *East West* (October 1987), 68–75. Information about the Collective was provided by its Women's Health Information Center, Box 192, West Somerville, MA 02144.

[39] Boston Women's Health Book Collective, *Our Bodies, Ourselves* (New York: Simon & Schuster, 1973); BWHBC, *The New Our Bodies, Ourselves* (New York: Simon & Schuster, 1985). The first *Our Bodies, Ourselves* sold close to 3 million copies in the United States and was translated into at least thirteen languages. BWHBC sells its books to health clinics and not-for-profit health organizations at a 70 percent discount.

and individual donations have helped launch new projects that empower women through shared information about health-related issues. Examples include recent books on teenage sexuality and the process of aging for women and a videotape on teenage pregnancy. Social surplus that might have been distributed to BWHBC members as financial reward for past work was instead used to fund expanded activity for the organization.

The BWHBC has shifted its organizational structure in ways that reflect elements of a more traditional board and staff model. Although its organizational structure is less collective, it has retained the term "collective" in its name, and it continues to allocate social surplus through democratic decision making.

Conclusion: A Sector of Alternatives?

The mix of institutions and organizations described here are commonly labeled a "third sector." Neither entirely public and governmental nor fully private and profit-seeking, these institutions exist in all societies. Some operate primarily in the world of markets, and others in the world of planned distribution of their services or products. Regardless of whether the third sector can be rigorously delineated as a cohesive part of the economy, discussions of development should give it more attention. First, these organizations have the potential to be highly responsive to local community needs. Many could have more democratically elected and more representative boards, as well as more democratic processes in their internal functions, than they now do. They do not exist to serve distant stockholders whose interests have to be met ultimately by extracting surplus from the community; neither do they function to meet the objectives of a distant governmental agency. Second, they can act as developers whose calculus includes a longer time frame and a different set of payoffs from those of most private firms. And compared to governmental agencies, they have the ability to amass social surplus for future development at a time when most governmental agencies are caught in a web of resistance to tax increases, calls for privatization of services, and escalating costs.

Alternative institutions draw opposition from various factions of capital. One reason is that capitalists sometimes miss the point that the net effect of nonprofit institutions has been to help maintain the system as it is. Without charitable organizations and service clubs, people would be more likely to question a system that cannot provide a living wage, or even jobs, to millions of the nation's people. In general, small businesses and locally based franchises are not blind to the constructive role of charitable organizations in the community, and many provide financial support for them. However, when proposals are made to transform charities into social services to which people have a right, business owners and managers feel threatened on two possible counts: They may have to pay part of the bill through taxes, and they may find fewer people willing to work for meager wages. Both have negative implications for profits.

Expanding noncharitable activities of third-sector organizations can also be threatening to local entrepreneurs. Small business people are a part of the fabric of a community. As long as they are providing goods or services at reasonable prices and levels of service, they minimize the likelihood that they will come into direct competition with new third-sector initiatives. Nevertheless, they may already be experiencing pressure from large corporate retailers or producers. Faced with the possibility that they will also have to compete with alternative organizations, they are likely to be vocal opponents.

As we have seen in the case of credit unions, the creation of alternatives may not threaten existing businesses, but fill segments of the market gladly relinquished or already abandoned. A primary health-care clinic organized as a cooperative, nonprofit venture in a rural area may simply provide a service that disappeared when retiring general practitioners could not find new physicians to take their places.

Planning for third-sector alternatives must be done with sensitivity to the important role played by small businesses in a community. Areas for development can be chosen by close attention to niches where services are absent or where major extraction of surplus from the community is taking place. Between those two situations considerable room remains for the entrepreneur to deliver goods and services at a reasonable price, create jobs, make a profit, and reinvest in the community.

By definition, mainstream organizations are reinforced and reproduced through normal social processes. They are supported by the state (through forms of regulation and maintenance of the legal commercial code), by educational institutions (from business-oriented curricula to general acculturation), and by other social institutions that reproduce society's values and ethics (religious institutions and the family). Part of the task of building an alternative or third sector of the economy entails development of institutions of support necessary to promote its growth and foster its development. Alternatives can become the norm only to the extent that they develop in conjunction with a set of symbiotic institutions, patterns of behavior, and values in society. We will return to this issue in Chapter 7.

Development of an alternative sector also necessitates constraining the prerogatives that mainstream institutions now enjoy. For development of community-based, more democratic economic activity, that means constraining capital. We turn now to a discussion of this issue.

5

Constraining Capital: Contentious Issues in Local Reforms

Reforms that modify capitalism have two basic attributes and an overall reference point. One attribute is the subject of this book: bringing greater amounts of social surplus under democratic control. Meaningful reforms also help to establish and sustain momentum for further change. They enlarge a juridical or popular base from which to work through outright increase in the strength of those working for progressive reform or through constraints imposed on those working against it. At the community level, imposing constraints on capital may be a first step. Constraints can allow the time necessary to articulate possible alternatives through public processes and to take action toward their realization.

The reference point is the other key element. The aim of reforms should not be simply to make a more humane capitalist system, desirable as that may be. From our perspective, reform efforts should be guided by a sense of a world beyond a restructured capitalism, one that is less exploitative of people and the earth. We will return to this issue in Chapter 7. In this chapter our focus is on practical and ideological barriers to reform at the local level.

Contentious Issues

In the day-to-day struggle for reform, routine rights and obligation, stagnation versus change, and choices of arenas and allies produce a reality that crowds out time for longer range strategic thinking, much less visions of an uncertain future. A host of contentious issues makes up a web in which debate over specific reforms takes place. One issue that we have discussed at length is social surplus. We begin this chapter on community action to constrain capital with a summary of six additional issues. Recognizing their presence should help community groups clarify their own thinking, better understand and prepare for their opposition, and pursue their goals more successfully.

The Public-Private Dichotomy

The issue of public versus private creates difficulty in organizing for local action in several ways. First and most general, ours is a privatized society relative to others. We have a strong tendency to understand social problems as problems of the individual and to treat them as private in nature. Our economic system, for example, produces increasing levels of unemployment from decade to decade as part of its normal functioning, yet the direct impact of the experience and the responses to the phenomenon—to deal with the economic deprivation of reduced income, to cope with the aura of guilt for being unemployed, to find a job—are essentially private. Unemployment insurance, public referral services, and retraining programs are partial public responses to the symptoms of the problem, but blame and necessary action for a "solution" lie with the individual and private-sector provision of jobs. There has been little social demand to forge changes in the organization of the economy that would eliminate the problem itself.

Through the public-private dichotomy real problems are mixed with perceptions shaped by image and ideology. In the past decade particularly, "public" has gained an image loaded with heightened pejorative elements of big government, ineptitude and inefficiency, and interference with freedom. The term "private" has more positive connotations of innovation, efficiency, and support for freedom. Over time, however, large public and private organizations share many of the same problems of a freedom-denying bureaucratic structure, lack of responsiveness, and occasional corruption. What gets lost as these images affect our lives is innovative thinking about and experimentation with alternatives, such as public but locally organized and controlled initiatives. At the community level need for goods and services often continues until the private entrepreneur chooses to respond, while segments of economic activity are cordoned off, figuratively and sometimes legally, as the domain of private initiative. This undercuts real material response by community groups that typically constitute themselves as public entities, and it limits imaginative quasi-public and collectively entrepreneurial responses to those needs through organizations such as community development corporations, cooperatives, and public-private joint ventures. The outcome is that surplus-generating opportunities are reserved for private profit and accumulation. Provision of goods and services that cannot generate surplus revenues becomes a public responsibility and starves for funding.

Analytically, the public-private dichotomy limits insight into the underlying causes of problems in the process of development itself. When private initiatives provide goods, services, jobs, and investment, attention is focused on how to design enticements necessary to bring about private action, rather than on strategies that could move various community-based organizations into more active roles.

Property Rights versus Social Rights

Communities have frequently had to deal with a fundamental conflict in our history—property rights versus social rights. Adapting the ideas of John Locke in his *Second Treatise of Civil Government* to the American Constitution led his "life, liberty and the pursuit of property" to be modified to "life, liberty and the pursuit of happiness." Some might suggest that in America today there is not much difference. Jefferson and others recognized the dilemma, but left it unresolved in constitutional prose. Today the dilemma surfaces in concrete form when communities confront rights assigned to owners of property, whether individuals or corporation as "legal individual." A firm's decision to close or move one of its facilities provides a relevant example. The private right to make such a decision can terminate a community's major source of employment. What rights does the community have in this situation? Legislative efforts designed to assure communities of even a few months' warning of such an event, much less the ability to delay or stop it, are difficult to enact because they are regarded as infringements on private rights of property, the rights to manage or dispose of it freely.[1] In a legal system geared to

[1] On the question of a community property right in the case of a plant shutdown by U.S. Steel, see Staughton Lynd, *The Fight against Shutdowns* (San Pedro, Calif., 1982), chap. 4. See also Staughton Lynd, "The Genesis of the Idea of a Community Right to Industrial Property in Youngstown and Pittsburgh, 1977–1987," *Journal of American History*, 74

private ownership of means of production, no distinction is made between personal and "productive" property. Privately owned personal property is generally not at issue. Privately owned property that serves as an essential element in the process whereby others make their livelihood—a factory, for instance—is very much at issue. Here, the rights of disposition, physical relocation, or destruction that are part of the package of rights of private property can threaten the health and well-being of entire communities. Social or public rights are only slowly being recognized and defined.

Communities do act to limit some forms of detrimental exercise of property rights. Zoning and land-use regulations address this issue but in often contradictory ways. These regulations are constantly challenged on the grounds that private property rights should take precedence over general perceptions of the public good. Communities use zoning laws as exclusionary devices to exclude those deemed undesirable because of race or class or to say no to industrial expansion or toxic waste. Zoning and land-use controls are elements of local control, and they can be shaped to serve progressive or reactionary ends. Fundamentally, however, they are at best prohibitive in nature; they do not provide grounds for substantive public initiative.[2]

The right of eminent domain enables government to take private property for public use with compensation to owners. Its basis is the superior power of the state over all land, and it has been used to assemble park land, rights of way for highways, and other reflections of publicly determined and legally constrained action for the public good. *Whose* good within society is often at question. Recent use of

---

(December 1987), 926–58. An employer and the Chamber of Commerce challenged as an infringement on federal pension law a law in the State of Maine that required severence pay for employees with at least three years of seniority in plants employing over one hundred which were closed or relocated. Maine's law was narrowly upheld by the U.S. Supreme Court (Fort Halifax Packing Co. v. Coyne, No. 86–341). Similar legislation under consideration in other states may gain momentum as a result of this ruling.

[2] For a provocative discussion on zoning and land-use controls, see Sidney Plotkin, *Keep Out: The Struggle for Land Use Control* (Berkeley, Calif., 1987). One recent challenge to land-use controls has succeeded through an important Supreme Court ruling. It establishes that "just compensation"—called for by the Fifth Amendment to the Constitution when private land is taken for public use—also applies when land-use regulation, implemented but then struck down by court action, has deprived owners of use of their property. While applicable to only a small number of cases, its impact will likely make state and local governments more cautious about new regulatory initiatives. See Robert Lindsey, "Decision May Put a Crimp on California's No-Growth Push," *New York Times*, June 14, 1987.

eminent domain to clear a Detroit neighborhood in order to make way for a new General Motors auto plant exemplifies this dilemma. Social rights can also be served by use of publicly and democratically controlled nongovernmental legal entities. For example, through land trusts controlled by locally elected boards, land is removed from market disposition, rights to its use are redefined, and it is held in long-term trust for a specific social use.

Perhaps the most profound social right in conflict with private rights emerges in the area of planning. Communities need to plan their futures—for energy needs or conservation, in order to maintain a clean environment or greenspace, to meet future residential or other needs. If those plans are to be more than exercises in collective wishful thinking, their action will interfere with the perceived property rights of individuals and corporations. If the social right to plan and act is to be assured, the legal system must find ways of resolving this conflict fairly, with reasonable compensation to those whose property rights are diminished but with a clearer conception of the right to act in the interest of a majority of citizens.

Individual, Interest Group, and Class

The individual as private actor was discussed in the first of these issues. In practical terms we can see a common tendency among people to operate alone, to take care of oneself, not interfering with or harming others, not tolerating tangible or symbolic injury to oneself or one's interests. Also in practical terms individuals can choose to ally with interest groups when it serves their aims. Thomas Hobbes, Jeremy Bentham, and other thinkers at the roots of the liberal tradition emphasized the value of the individual personality and saw it as a set of capacities which the individual "owns" free and clear of any debt to society. The social sciences make extensive use of individualist models, even when attempting to model social activity.

Interest groups can be the practical means of organizing for group action in a large and diverse society. They enable people to overcome the costs of organizing, to gain attention in public processes, and to have an impact on decisions. They are central to a pluralist conception of politics in which the state is a neutral arena for policy-making. Policy results from the interplay of shifting autonomous wills of individuals as reflected through interest groups and parties. This way of thinking shares attributes of the equilibrium market model in economics, and some of its mechanistic and ahistorical foundations as well.[3]

The concept of class is often neglected. The idea that groups of people share common interests and objectives that stem from their roles in material production is foreign to much of contemporary social science. In the pluralist model, labor becomes just another interest group, and capital disappears entirely. In real life, communities are often accurately defined by class determinants. Residents share common bonds because they own means of production or alternatively because they work for those who do. Community patterns of communication and action are influenced by experiences such as participation in labor unions or social interaction at private clubs. Class-based issues are significant to an informed analysis of local development, as well as to shaping action to affect its form and substance.

Plan and Market

Plan and market refer to multiple institutions and mechanisms by which production and distribution of goods and services are accomplished. In most situations, concrete activities fall on a continuum between the two worlds conjured up by these two terms. The plan-market dichotomy is not limited to debates over economic systems; it often lurks beneath the surface of discussion of what can and should be done in terms of economic development at the local level. It is also frequently posited in simplistic terms, as if a pure form of either plan or market is desirable, attainable, or both. In reality pure examples are hard to find.

Planning is done by private individuals, by for-profit and not-for-profit firms, and by quasi-public organizations and public agencies.[4] All plan in the sense of setting goals and devising strategies to meet them. What distinguishes planning of this type is that it is not done, directly and specifically, to allocate privately produced goods and

[3] See Anthony Downs, *An Economic Theory of Democracy* (New York, 1957), and Randall Bartlett, *Economic Foundations of Political Power* (New York, 1973).

[4] The world has not held planning in high esteem in the 1980s, but good work on planning theory and technique has continued regardless. See, for example, John Forester, *Planning in the Face of Power* (Berkeley, Calif., 1989), and John Friedmann, *Knowledge and Action: Mapping the Planning Theory Domain* (Princeton, N.J., 1987). Practical treatment of planning is promised in Norman Krumholz and John Forester, *Making Equity Planning Work: Leadership in the Public Sector* (Philadelphia, forthcoming).

services. Planning is done for production of these commodities, for their distribution to wholesale or retail outlets; and it is done in order to encourage sales. Final distribution comes about by the consumer's choice in the retail market. For the household doing the buying this may be a planned rather than a spontaneous purchase, and the producer may count on the sale with varying degrees of certainty or uncertainty, but the final disposition is not an act planned by the producer.

Compared to other wealthy Western capitalist societies, the economy of the United States makes extensive use of market transactions in the disposition of goods and services. The U.S. government taxes away a lower percentage of individual and business income to pay for planned collective consumption of publicly provided goods and services; more is available for private expenditure, limiting the needs for public planning in the routine operation of the economy.[5]

To encourage greater amounts of community-based action on development is to encourage more planning. For reasons outlined in all of these issues, movement in that direction is not easy to foster. It will be perceived as time consuming, as most public and democratic process is, and it will be deemed worthwhile only if it leads to desired and concrete results. Setting goals and planning strategy to meet them are part of the battle; organizing for effective community action is another.

Centralization versus Decentralization

Pursuit of greater local initiative in an era of accelerating international interdependency seems paradoxical. In many ways global interdependency shifts the locus of decision making to the national level, reinforcing demands for a strong central state to do battle for international "competitive advantage." Through this phenomenon the federalist argument for the United States is called further into question, and corporatist strategies gain favor.[6] A frequently quoted concern

[5] One measure that allows international comparison of this phenomenon is government receipts as a percent of gross national product. The United States, Britain, and Italy have recently been in the range of 30–40 percent by this measure, with the U.S. at the low end of the group. Those at the top among Western industrial countries include Sweden, the Netherlands, and Denmark, all around 50 percent. See *National Accounts of OECD Countries, 1964–1981*, Vol. 2 (Paris: Organization for Economic Cooperation and Development, 1982).

[6] Arguments for industrial policy tend to fit this mold. See, for example, Felix G. Rohatyn, "Time for a Change," *New York Review of Books*, August 18, 1983, pp. 46–49.

for the "governability of democracy" cautions the nation regarding problems created by interest groups clammering for attention at the national level.[7] National politics should, it would seem, be left to the experts. Another version of a strong central government argument is more narrowly defined—back to the basics of national defense and general management of the economy. But it too holds little place for an active citizenry engaged in the national process of governance; citizen involvement is limited to voting for representatives and a symbol-laden president. Other central players, such as high court judges, key bureaucrats, and managers of the money supply, are appointed. This vision of government promises to allow more room for governance at the local level, such as maintaining social programs and chartering corporations. But who are the appropriate parties to take part in local governance, and how do they develop material and human resources with which to work? Under this model, decentralized power has usually been held by those with economic resources, typically white males from privileged backgrounds. Decentralization of this kind, with little debate and citizen involvement, can also be accompanied by a narrowing of the sense of community, yielding a parochialism and a suffocating tyranny of uniformity. Countering Rousseau's optimism, John Stuart Mill warned of this outcome in *On Liberty*.

A positive outcome of centralization in governance is the ability to set minimum standards for social and economic activity and to share the resources to achieve them; to reduce costs of building and maintaining infrastructure; and to maintain relations within the international arena. The desired ends of decentralization are shifting collective decision making to the lowest administrative unit possible to facilitate fuller citizen participation; reducing the institutions of life to a more human scale and countering bureaucratic tendencies in them; and encouraging diversity in communities within acceptable limits of material well-being and social justice.

Decentralization offers conceptual and practical alternatives if it is wedded to redistributive policies that shift national resources from wealthy to less wealthy communities. These policies can be accompanied by enforcement of central standards for basic rights and for access to basic material needs. Centralization provides uniform min-

[7] The phrase is Samuel Huntington's. See Michael J. Crozier, Samuel P. Huntington, and Joji Watanuki, *The Crisis of Democracy* (New York, 1975), pp. 114–15.

imum standards and some resources; decentralization then opens areas for greater citizen involvement in decision making at the local level and for the innovation that can result from that involvement.

Representative Democracy and Direct Democracy

Models of direct democratic practice have been marginalized by many contemporary thinkers as artifacts of a simpler age. They do not fit well with corporatist-liberal conceptions of the future or with resurgent conservative thinking. To liberals, the rationale for representative forms of democracy lies in the complexity of the governance process, the need for trained and experienced full-time participants, the awesome scale of the issues and dollars involved. To conservatives, broad-based participatory democracy is countered by an orthodoxy that is elitist; ordinary citizens are unable to play an effective role in governance beyond occasionally casting votes for society's most extraordinary leaders. In this view, extraordinariness traditionally resulted from being from the best of families (and white and male); in its more modern form, extraordinariness results from a meritocratic selection process of education, corporate leadership, and (perhaps) public office.

Direct democracy draws its spirit and content from the work of Rousseau, and from Jefferson and Dewey in its American tradition. Citizens take direct responsiblity for informing themselves of issues, discussing them, and voting on them. They are engaged in the process of governance on an ongoing basis, along with their routine callings. Representatives in this form of governance are kept in close contact with their constituency, they serve a limited number of terms in office, and they are subject to recall. Citizen participation is the key; people are routinely involved in some aspects of self-governance as both their right and responsibility. They do so not out of special qualification or knowledge, but as part of a committed, public life. Conflicts in life are expected, and transformative in that they must ultimately be resolved by innovation and compromise. Citizens are educated to take part in governance and receive further education through their participation.[8] Wherever possible, people are directly engaged in the process of making public decisions and plans.

[8] This argument is basic to much of the writing of Jean-Jacques Rousseau, John Stuart Mill, and Alexis de Tocqueville. For contemporary elaborations, see Carole Pateman, *Participation and Democratic Theory* (Cambridge, 1970), chap. 2, and Benjamin Barber, *Strong Democracy: Participatory Politics for a New Age* (Berkeley, Calif., 1984), chap. 9.

The list above summarizes many of the contentious issues that must be addressed in making sense of community action for development. They have been treated separately for clarity, but they generally confront us together as a sense of "reality" or the possible. Each of us uses these issues as an important part of the framework that helps us to understand the world. We shape and partly compose our world view or ideology according to these issues. In our work on community-based economic development, we emphasize particular aspects—many times those more neglected in theory and practice—of each of these dichotomies. Taken together these issues do not constitute a full field of inquiry for this study; surely we have neglected some of a general nature and others that may become important in specific instances of community action.

One more significant issue, appropriation of social surplus, must be included in the list. Discussion of social surplus is contentious in itself, and it is affected by several of these other issues. Does it accrue to public or private coffers? Is its appropriation simply a right of property ownership, or are there social rights involved? What individuals, interest groups, or classes are served by its creation and appropriation? Our discussion of locally based efforts to constrain capital and the ways they involve these issues follows.

Rent Control

Housing is such a basic need and so poorly met for so many that the lack of affordable housing has forced some constraints on capital. A third of the nation's population lives in rental housing that is owned either by private landlords or public housing authorities.[9] The cost of their housing is affected by supply-side considerations (the local housing stock, its condition, the percentage of vacant housing) and demand-side characteristics (income level of perspective renters, growth or decline in their numbers, the availability of other options

[9] The figure commonly cited for home ownership in the United States is that two-thirds of all households live in homes they own. The difficulty that young, moderate-income families have had in entering the market as buyers, however, has reduced that figure. For instance, for people 30 to 34 years old, home ownership rates fell from 61.1 percent in 1980 to 53 percent in 1987. See "The State of the Nation's Housing," Joint Center for Housing Studies, Harvard University, March 1988.

in housing). Tenants under pressure to pay higher rents can turn to their employers for higher pay, or they can organize to gain public control over the rate at which rents can be increased. The stagnation of real wages has contributed to renewed interest in controlling rents, an action normally taken at the local level.

Given the choice and given the world as it is, most Americans would prefer to own their residences. Ownership provides a modicum of control over this important site of life activities, it provides a cushion against the financial uncertainties of labor markets and a crisis-prone economy, and it can provide an opportunity to save with a potentially high payoff through price appreciation. The fact that fewer families can pursue this component of the American dream has been routinely reported in recent years. Escalating prices relative to real incomes take their toll on those not already in ownership positions. Some might logically seek out alternatives. However, because of the paucity of mutual, co-op, and municipal housing in this country compared to many others, they have instead fed a sustained and growing demand for existing rental housing stock. Urban gentrification and rising building costs have contributed to landlords' ability to push rents upward. People need shelter, and they can be forced to pay a higher price for it when alternative housing services are unavailable.

Rent control is a direct attempt to constrain returns to capital invested in housing. It is a form of regulation that can be imposed locally only if the political strength can be mustered to bring it about. In areas of fast-rising rental rates and numerous renters, this political issue can gain broad popular support. It will also bring out a vast array of opposition. Even local employers, whose self-interest could lead them to support a measure that would take some pressure off wage demands, remain unsupportive out of fear for the broader implications of price controls in the provision of a major consumer service.

A small city that successfully imposed rent control in the late 1970s is Santa Monica, California. Middle-class retirees and moderate-income residents not already driven out by escalating housing costs provided the base for a tenents' movement that resulted in a political shake-up of city government.[10] In 1981, with a progressive majority on the city council, further measures to control growth were enacted.

[10] The selling price of a Santa Monica home between September 1988 and March 1989 was close to $700,000; see Kenneth J. Garcia, "Buying a Home in Boomtown," *Los Angeles*

Santa Monica's rent-control law applies to all apartments except those in owner-occupied buildings of three rental units or less. It allows annual rent increases, and landlords may petition for special increases to cover unusual costs of maintenance. An elected, independent rent-control board with its own legal staff administers the law, which courts at local and state levels have upheld against extensive challenges. A strong tenant ownership rights act, a supplement adopted by special municipal election in 1984, specifies controls on the conversion of rental units to condominiums and stipulates a tax to be paid on all conversions except those to limited equity housing units. This Tenant Participation Conversion Tax is equal to a year's rent on the unit. Proceeds of the tax are used to provide housing for low-, moderate-, and middle-income households as defined in terms of the median gross income for Los Angeles County. A late 1987 study of the impact of rent controls on Santa Monica's tenants indicated stability in the size of rental housing stock, increased length of residence of renters, relatively stable maintenance, and fewer tenant-landlord disputes. Rent controls were estimated to be saving residents an average of $159 per month relative to other renters in Los Angeles County and to be maintaining rental rates in controlled units of approximately 30 percent of household income.[11]

Rent control has been combined with controls on other forms of development in the city. A six-month moratorium on all construction led to a suit against the city by the local carpenters' union.[12] Downtown high-rise office development was constrained. New development was approved with quid pro quos: small business space at sidewalk

Times, March 19, 1989. See also Derek Shearer, "Planning and the New Urban Populism: The Case of Santa Monica, California," *Journal of Planning Education and Research* 2 (Summer 1982), 20–26, and "How Progressives Won in Santa Monica," *Social Policy* 12 (1982), 7–14. Later assessment of the Santa Monica experience can be found in Mark E. Kann, "Radicals in Power: Lessons from Santa Monica," *Socialist Review* (May–June 1983), 81–101, and *Middle Class Radicalism in Santa Monica* (Philadelphia, 1986); and Pierre Clavel, *The Progressive City: Planning and Participation 1969–1984* (New Brunswick, N.J., 1986), chap. 5.

[11] Santa Monica's rent control ordinance (available from the Rent Control Administration, City Hall, 1685 Main Street, Santa Monica, CA 90401) is reprinted in John I. Gilderbloom et al., *Rent Control: A Sourcebook* (Santa Barbara, Calif., 1981), 303–17. The Tenant Participation Conversion Tax is specified in Santa Monica Charter, Tenant Ownership Rights, Article 20, June 26, 1984. Assessment of the impact of Santa Monica's rent control is provided in Ned Levine, J. Eugene Grisby III, and Allan Heskin, "Who Benefits from Rent Control? Effects on Tenants in Santa Monica, California," *Journal of the American Planning Association* 56 (Spring 1990), 140–52.

[12] Shearer, "Planning and the New Urban Populism," p. 22.

levels; commitments to build low-income housing if luxury high-rises were approved; underground parking; space for daycare included in office buildings. Citizen task forces and neighborhood groups advised the city council on mixed-use development, revitalization of a stagnating downtown mall area, and development of the Santa Monica Pier.

Rent control leaves the private provision of rental housing in place and attempts to control its price. If it is to be used successfully, rent control requires rethinking how housing will be provided. When capital's profit is constrained in this market, it will move elsewhere.[13] Santa Monica has acted slowly in developing limited equity co-ops and other municipally sponsored housing. Its housing agency and community corporation have been hampered in part by a lack of available land. They have developed plans to make use of air rights over five municipal parking lots. One will provide two stories of parking and four stories for seventy-two units of senior-citizen housing; another will provide parking plus forty-nine units of moderate-income housing. The dedicated housing fund from the Tenant Participation Conversion Tax is generating approximately $150,000 per year in equity for this activity, which helps leverage federal and state funds for housing.[14] Rent control can constrain capital in one segment of the housing market and keep a basic need more affordable for some community residents.

Rent Control and Contentious Issues in Reform

The attempt to control rental prices of housing involves public intervention in what is generally considered a private process between landlords and renters. Rent control recognizes some degree of social rights to affordable housing. In a case of escalating housing prices, it is one means by which a community acts to assure that people of moderate or lower income can continue to live in the community.

[13] The economics textbook argument against rent control is persuasive only in the narrow context of assumption about a free-market, private-enterprise economy. There the "artificially low," less-than-market clearing price set by rent control will leave a gap between the amount of housing consumers demand and the quantity that private investors will be willing to supply. Most textbooks never address the possibility that this gap could be closed by municipal, mutual, or co-op forms of housing, or that housing might not be treated as a commodity supplied through the market.

[14] Interview with Candy Rupp, housing program manager, City of Santa Monica, March 20, 1989.

Both of these rights create conflict with the property rights of owners of rental housing to set the rental price.

Rent control pits what are often thought of as interest groups—tenants and landlords—against one another. In class terms, it can be seen as regulation of the conflictive relationship between the interest of property-owning capitalists, attempting to maximize the rental flow from their property, and people who do not own residential property, typically wage earners or pensioners.

Markets for rental housing, and housing services in general, can be modified by rent control. Imposition of rent control may curtail private planning for construction of new rental housing and hasten the need for public or quasi-public planning for its provision. It is a decentralized and municipal, rather than state or national, action. Developers and landlords have tried to block it at the state level in California and elsewhere. Efforts to move beyond rent control to various forms of social provision of housing require accumulation of resources at all levels of governance and, ideally, decentralized planning, construction, and control of actual housing.

Before rent control can be enacted into law by representatives in city government, it must be encouraged and fought for through citizen action. Its administration can provide the opportunity for rotating citizen participation on rent-control boards and direct involvement in neighborhood associations. Rent control can lead to some degree of community control over the amount of social surplus extraction through rent. But surplus remains privately appropriated, and its reinvestment remains a private decision. It may leave the community or the housing sector.

Controlling Growth

Few people have difficulty in thinking of reasons why at least some forms of economic growth should be controlled in their community. Debates over controlling growth have to do with kinds of growth, extent of control, and what means of control to use.

The paradox of controlling growth is quite clear. Rate of growth is the primary indicator of economic health that we use. We think of the national economy as experiencing a good year if its growth rate is over 3 percent. On the other hand, communities often set growth limits. While few of them can afford a no-growth position, many have opted for slow growth. One of the reasons for the paradox lies in failure to distinguish between economic growth (crudely measured by indicators such as gross national product) and economic development. Growth implies more of the same. Development points to changing relationships between people and their environment, changing institutions, and perhaps new criteria for what is deemed good or bad in life.[15] Many communities wrestling with growth control have reached a level of affluence that enables them to work on the question of how to pursue development, not just growth. The challenge is to encourage more communities to become innovative about development at an earlier stage of growth.

Specifying limits on growth means making increasingly fine distinctions among kinds of development. For example, local ordinances that were once written with simple definitions of residential, commercial, and industrial activities have proven anachronistic. Today communities make distinctions between office developments, transportation facilities, and light, medium, and heavy industry. Commercial development in highway strips versus malls and downtown malls versus peripheral mall locations can be specified. In deciding which kinds of growth to encourage or discourage, communities carefully weigh taxes, traffic impact, the nature of jobs created, amenities required, environmental pollution, and other factors. They establish controls and incentives for growth they consider desirable, or they construct the controls and incentives in an ad hoc fashion in response to particular new investment proposals. It is unlikely that the Chicago suburb of Hoffman Estates had a policy in place in its ordinances which suited the needs of Sears, Roebuck and Company. But when Sears sought a new location for its corporate headquarters, Hoffman Estates responded. In conjunction with the State of Illinois, it offered nearly a quarter of a billion dollars in incentives.[16] On a state or

[15] We are indebted to Richard Schramm of the Urban Studies and Planning Department, Massachusetts Institute of Technology, for encouraging us to make this important distinction.

[16] The State of Illinois assembled a package for Sears's Hoffman Estates location that included $62 million in site preparation, highways, and tax breaks, and the additional incentive of a tax increment financing (TIF) district, an arrangement whereby twenty years of Sears's local property tax payments will be used to pay off bonds issued to acquire the site. That will be worth an additional $178 million to Sears. These incentives were deemed necessary not because Hoffman Estates was a poor community seeking rapid growth, but because Sears was also being enticed to relocate to North Carolina and Texas. See David Moberg, "This Sears Sale Item Is Not in the Catalogue," *In These Times*, August 2–29, 1989, 6.

perhaps even a national level, this marked a new record in subsidies per job. No quid pro quos were extracted in exchange for this public giveaway; the appeal of approximately six thousand people working on a new office and transport campus was enough. Hoffman Estates would no doubt have rejected a steel mill, or perhaps even an automotive assembly operation, of the same scale.

Boulder, Colorado, chose to control growth in other ways. It has rejected at least one large, "high-tech" manufacturing facility because it would have been located on land designated as greenbelt. Early in the era of setting constraints on growth, Boulder managed to restrict carefully the location of housing development in the city and on nearby mountain terrain.[17] Counting greenspace as an asset for all residents, Boulder has been relatively consistent in blocking exceptions.

In addition to kinds of growth and extent of control, the means used to control growth is another debatable dimension. Impact fees are controversial means to discourage growth and to assure that a larger portion of the cost of growth is met by developers or new commercial or residential occupants than in the past. They are crude instruments because they raise costs for developers and their customers, and those who can pay higher prices simply pay them. Impact fees extend the range of costs to developers from traditional charges for roads or sewers to other municipal services necessary to growth. Widening or rebuilding area roads, building a new fire station or a new school, providing resources to develop a daycare facility, or general fees to cover the cost of expanding a police force are examples of the costs being assigned to new development projects. Since these fees are voted into existence by local residents and borne by residents-to-be, they are relatively easy to enact. Developers and real estate interests fight them at both the local and state levels. Some oppose them as exclusionary, whereas others argue that they provide the only means by which growth can continue. Without these fees, it is feared that local residents would enact strict no-growth measures. The conservative columnist George Will has noted the paradox of impact fees in staunchly free-market areas of the country; he labels this kind of control "Sunbelt Bolshevism."[18]

[17] See Chapter 6 for a discussion of Boulder's planned development of open public land.

[18] George Will, "Californians Resort to Slow-Growth Laws," *Ithaca Journal*, December 15, 1987.

Wal-Mart

Constraining capital's locational choice is often a matter of trying to steer growth, rather than merely attempting to slow it down. Communities facing development of a shopping mall on their periphery can look to probable declines in older town or city-center commercial activity, as well as increased costs of providing services to an outlying site. Strip development is inefficient in terms of parking, land use, water and sewer connections, and difficulty of service from public transit. Well-designed malls overcome some, but not all, of these problems. Smaller rural towns rarely face the prospect of full-blown mall development, but they are often targets for mini-malls initiated and anchored by discount stores. These projects are purposely located outside areas with zoning restrictions, where large parcels of moderately priced land are to be found.

Wal-Mart's practice has been to gain quietly an option to buy a parcel of land contiguous to an incorporated town. Terms for the purchase include winning the town's agreement to annex the land and to provide water and sewer service. The landowner, often a local resident, and the local realtor who stands to make a substantial commission if the sale goes through become the team that promotes the deal with advice and counsel from Wal-Mart. The town is attracted by the prospect of tax revenues from a store that will draw buyers from the surrounding area, even though its own downtown businesses will be the losers.

Independence, Iowa, has gone through this transition. In 1985, the first full year of operation, its Wal-Mart did $10 million in business. Yet total retail sales for the town, including the annexed Wal-Mart development, were up only $2.1 million. What did this change mean to the people of Independence? Other merchants in town took a beating. Area shoppers got lower prices, probably some gain in selection of goods, and the convenience of one-stop shopping, but they lost personal service and the ability to walk easily to the shopping site. The town gained some tax revenue, although more would have been lost if Wal-Mart had made good on its threat to locate in a nearby town. Legal and insurance needs of Wal-Mart were met from their corporate headquarters, rather than by local attorneys and brokers. Wal-Mart's cash receipts moved through the local bank very quickly, providing little in added revenue there. Almost as many jobs were lost in other businesses as were created. In sum, area small businesses have lost significant social surplus to Wal-Mart stockholders.[19] Independence and its neighboring towns are left with moribund downtowns. For Independence, this may be growth, but it is not necessarily development. For the area, it is neither.

Regional and national developers such as Wal-Mart have had it easy because so much of the nation's land-use control is only local. However, county, region, and state cooperation in designing controls is increasing. The State of Vermont provides an example. Periods of speculative price increases had removed the teeth from the 1973 Land Gains Tax that punished short-term ownership with a 60 percent tax on land sold after it was held less than a year. The tax diminished in percentage until it was eliminated on land held longer than six years. Developers who carved up rural land for vacation home sites were able simply to pay the tax, passing it on in the price of lots sold to buyers from high-income areas of the country. In addition, the state building code regulation offered little protection in terms of what was built. The Growth Management Act of 1988 (Act 200) was designed to balance Vermont's tradition of home rule with the need to take better account of the regional impact of larger development projects.[20] Implementation of the law is in the hands of the Department of Housing and Community Affairs. Every town is to be part of a regional commission and has the opportunity to participate in designing its regional plan. The State Council of Regional Commissions uses statewide criteria to review the plan. Approval at the state level is required before land-use permits for large-scale projects are issued. This arrangement is designed to encourage local planning; town plans have been rare in Vermont, but now, without an approved local plan, the regional plan will take precedence.

Vermonters concerned about preserving local autonomy and the property rights of individuals have not taken kindly to Act 200. Some towns have refused to participate in its process, and a statewide group called Citizens for Property Rights has been formed to encourage

[19] Jon Bowermaster, "When Wal-Mart Comes to Town," *New York Times Magazine-Business World*, April 2, 1989, pp. 67, 68. Wal-Mart stockholders include Sam Walton, Wal-Mart's founder and the country's richest man until he began dividing his money among his family.

[20] The full name of Vermont's law is Vermont Municipal and Regional Planning and Development Act, as amended by the 1988 Growth Management Act (Act 200), Title 24 Vermont Statutes Annotated Chapter 117, July 1988.

others to do the same. The outcome of this political contest remains unclear.

Constraining capital's ability to pursue growth can take grass-roots, issue-oriented form. In Boulder, Colorado, for instance, an environmentally concerned local planning group helped shape development of a mall (discussed in Chapter 6). In San Antonio, Texas, COPS (Communities Organized for Public Service), a citizen action group of moderate-income, Mexican-American members, tackles growth issues regularly. In an unusually early conceptual linkage between the environmental impact of new development and the cost of living for San Antonio residents, COPS joined the battle against constructing a shopping mall over the Edwards Aquifer, the city's source of drinking water. Their fear was that new pollution from parking lot runoff and elimination of recharge capacity in the aquifer would create need for new purification plants, thereby raising the cost of water.[21] COPS was instrumental in turning out for a referendum a large group of voters opposed to the mall. Since that victory, COPS has worked to capture public funds for redevelopment of existing city neighborhoods. Efforts have included blocking "subsidized" development on the city's north side; expansion caused increases in utility rates to finance extension of services there. Free materials were provided to developers for installation of water mains when the city's residents in poorer neighborhoods were faced with deteriorating water lines.[22] Growth can still take place in outlying, largely white and more affluent areas, but developers and new residents will not have as much access to tax revenues from city residents to hasten and subsidize the process.

Growth Control and Contentious Issues in Reform

Controlling growth inhibits capital in particular ways. It represents one way in which public decisions set constraints on the pursuit of private self-interest and economic gain. As an exercise of social rights to limit growth—especially economic growth—in their pace, location,

[21] See Chapter 4, note 16, for literature on COPS. For an analysis of the aquifer confrontation, see Sidney Plotkin, "Democratic Change in the Urban Political Economy: San Antonio's Edwards Aquifer Controversy," in *The Politics of San Antonio,* Johnson, Booth, and Harris, eds., pp. 157–74.

[22] Joseph D. Sekul, "Communities Organized for Public Service: Citizen Power and Public Policy in San Antonio," in ibid., pp. 175–90.

or form, it constrains rights that are typically assigned to property owners.

Efforts to control or shape growth are contentious in part because they involve conflicting interests and class outcomes. Growth control can be used to protect the special ambiance of an affluent community or to promote the interests of one faction of a class over another (real estate versus industrial capital; office workers versus industrial workers).

Growth control may constrain markets, but it is not necessarily a form of planning. If substantive goals can be identified, controls can be wedded to indicative planning to encourage their outcome (e.g., tax breaks for cluster housing that preserves open areas) or more direct planning and execution (e.g., construction of a certain number of units per year of municipal-based, tenant-run housing).

One of the shortcomings of local growth control measures is that their jurisdiction ends at the border of the community enacting them. Vermont's new planning process, designed to foster local planning linked to regional plans under guidelines set at the state level, constitutes one means of maintaining decentralized initiative in controlling growth while incorporating it into a broader spatial logic and set of values. Citizen involvement in sorting out means and ends for controls is essential but often missing. Town meetings, neighborhood councils, recall of representatives, referendums, and open citizen action groups can assure that voices are heard.

Setting controls on growth necessarily favors or limits different groups in their accumulation of social surplus. Controls affect what new activities can be introduced, or which existing ones can be expanded. Generally the issue of whether surplus will continue to be appropriated privately is not addressed.

State Banking Regulation

Concentration and centralization of capital are basic features of capitalism missed by Adam Smith in his early appraisal of the economic system. Today we are awash in a new wave of both trends. Mergers and acquisitions and the growth of firms already in oligopolistic positions in one or more industries are routine occurrences. These phenomena have been especially prevalent in banking and financial services.

What has been referred to as the thrift industry is in precipitous decline. The cost to the average taxpayer of the misguided deregulation of the savings and loan segment of the industry continues to escalate. It is bitter icing on the cake of the Reagan-Bush era's redistribution to the wealthy. The savings and loan bailout may well lead to a stripped-down and consolidated group of lending institutions operating under renewed federal scrutiny with less local control. At the same time, banks are engaged in mergers, broadening of services, and geographic expansion. Recent years have brought a steady weakening of the Glass-Steagall Act of 1933, the post-crash regulation that has kept banks out of Wall Street-type underwriting. Entry of other financial institutions into portions of banks' former activities means that banks will compete head-on with large American financial conglomerates, brokerage firms, and insurance companies. Interstate expansion has accelerated. In addition, all of these firms will feel increasing pressure from even larger foreign firms hoping to move further into the American market. Sharp price competition may ensure stability for a while, but the Darwinian competition among giants will leave a residue of closed or swallowed-up regional, state, and local institutions in its trail. States and localities have not stopped this process. At the local level, communities may be able to extract promises of behavior becoming good corporate citizens, such as maintaining service throughout a city. A carrot-and-stick approach could mean bartering over deposit of locally controlled assets such as governmental funds and pensions.

At the state level, sound regulation may be more feasible. The State of Maine provides an example of defensive action in an attempt to block drainage of funds from banks that could result from outside take-overs. Maine has instituted a "Net New Funds" regulation that requires any financial institution or financial holding company with intentions to acquire more than 5 percent of voting shares in a Maine-based bank to make a binding commitment to bring new funds into the state.[23] New funds can take the form of initial capital investment; loan, dividend, or investment policies; or a plan to expand consumers'

[23] We are indebted to Roxanne Ward Zaghab, formerly with the National Center for Policy Alternatives (NCPA), for bringing this action to our attention and educating us on other initiatives on banking. See NCPA's Regulatory Summary, "Maine Net New Funds Regulation," photocopy (n.d.), available from the National Center for Policy Alternatives, 2000 Florida Avenue, Washington, DC 20009.

service needs. The regulation also limits the payout to stockholders during the acquiring bank's first ten years in the state, and gives the state banking superintendent broad access to bank records.

In Maine supporters count on the Department of Business Regulation of the Bureau of Banking to promulgate and enforce these regulations. Advocates for this new agency must continue to propose legislation to safeguard state residents' interests with regard to other banking services and investment policies. Other states have these powers as well. Although it may be costly for regional, national, or international banks to comply with state laws, they leave some degree of control in the states' hands. States can tailor bank action to meet the needs of their residents and businesses and to extract compliance in exchange for the right to do business there. Disclosure laws (stronger state versions of the federal Community Reinvestment Act), obligatory bank lending to state funds for economic development, and requirements that specific volumes of loans be made for specific purposes (e.g., long-term business loans) are examples of reform by aggressive state regulatory agencies. Banks, however, continue to operate as private institutions that can have dramatic effect on the well-being of the communities and states in which they operate. By the pricing of their services and the spreads they charge in lending, they will continue to appropriate social surplus into private hands.

State Regulation of Banking and Contentious Issues in Reform

Most private activity takes place within parameters set by public law or custom, and banking is no exception. Debate hinges on the degree to which a public voice intervenes in, or constrains, private business decision making. In debates over bank regulation, the rights of private stockholders and their managers to take action to enhance the magnitude of their property holdings are pitted against the social right to protection from the harmful effects of power exercised through property ownership. Access to capital and financial services is essential to modern life; it is a basic community need. How that need will be met, and the private rights exercised in meeting it, are at issue.

State regulation is designed to protect individual citizens and businesses from the power of large corporate entities and to assure smooth delivery of goods or services for businesses and consumers. Regulation must also be understood in class terms. By the time it is enacted, it often serves the interest of the industry it is designed to regulate. In its most progressive form, it shifts power from capital to a broader mix of community members.

Some forms of regulation impose planned outcomes that a market system would not assure. The quid pro quos extracted by state regulators often help fill areas of "market failure," such as a state's dearth of risk capital or funds available for loans to minority-owned businesses. State and even city regulation of banking means decentralized controls compared to federal regulation, and they allow customized regulation to meet local needs. Banks and financial institutions, increasingly national and global, would surely rather not have to keep track of and try to control regulatory activity across fifty states and numerous major cities.

Bank regulation at the state level takes place from both agency mandate and legislation. Most regulators are appointed subject to legislative approval. The approval process as well as debate over regulations allow some opportunity for citizen group and voter involvement. In general, implementation of regulatory processes is under representative oversight.

State regulation of banking may slow the rate of banks' surplus extraction from the state, but it does not change the fundamental ability of capital to deploy in search of surplus value or its ultimate appropriation by private owners of banks. Stemming concentration and centralization of capital in this industry or the economy is unlikely.

Local Reforms and Local Small Business

Local entrepreneurs and small-business people are essential to a community's vitality. In the same way that a locally owned, independent restaurant can do more for a community than a McDonald's, local business developers are more likely than nonlocal developers to purchase goods and services and reinvest locally. Managing the contradictions inherent in dealing with this constituency is one of the toughest tasks facing a community struggling with reforms.

Compared to outside developers, local entrepreneurs have a broader array of formal rights and informal techniques that can be used to win approval of their plans. They can credibly argue for their projects based on their concern for the community. They can pressure friends or neighbors who may serve on crucial boards, or they can rally groups such as the local Chamber of Commerce to their support. They also have the option of running for office on the city council or the zoning board or of supporting candidates who they know are sympathetic to the kind of development they have in mind.

Controlling growth is a constant source of conflict between local government and entrepreneurs. Most reforms are viewed as restricting entrepreneurial freedom, but some can make new opportunities apparent. Plans that have won popular support can incorporate entrepreneurs rather than fight them. The planning process itself can highlight community needs to which local developers can respond. Public-private partnerships can help realize planned objectives while opening new opportunities to tap the skills and energy of a community's entrepreneurial residents. The ultimate attraction that a community engaged in development provides to past and prospective local business people is the promise of a vital environment and healthy economy in which to do business.

6

Creating Public Assets

Our strategy for development runs against the grain of capitalism. In the most general sense, it would shift resources away from the private sector and employ all means possible to assure that democratic processes are followed in putting resources to use under public control.

Two points require attention with this discussion. The first involves the host of problems normally associated with publicly or socially held resources. The common question—but who *really* owns them?—summarizes deep concern that responsible stewardship requires the exercise of private property rights. We think that examples used in this book do not support that assumption, but it would be foolish to ignore numerous instances in which accountability is lost, bureaucracy impedes effective administration, or political staffing overloads an organization with ineffective personnel. A good deal has been learned about what makes for effective public stewardship and enterprise. The limited experiences of the United States can be augmented by a deep literature from Western Europe and the ongoing debates on how to restructure the economies of Eastern Europe. Especially significant to community-based public assets is the experience of municipal socialism in England. Before being derailed by the Thatcher government, city administrators in Sheffield and London made enough progress in decentralized municipalization to provide both positive and negative new lessons. In the United States a legacy of effective city administrations by "water and sewer socialists" provides another record to be scrutinized for keys to success and failure.[1]

[1] An excellent summary of lessons from recent municipal experience in England can be

The second issue may seem obvious, but we will make it explicit. The initiatives we review here are local and community based. We do not address statewide institutions such as the Bank of North Dakota or regional-federal ventures such as the Tennessee Valley Authority. Neither will we address the issue of public take-over of failing firms, a complex issue worthy of its own in-depth study.[2]

The tax system funds routine expenditures of the public sector, but how does a community move beyond this regular stream of income to build new foundations for development? Annual budget surpluses are not likely to appear in the near future at the federal level, and they are becoming increasingly rare at the state and local levels. Decision makers operating in the public realm face extreme difficulty meeting routine financial commitments. Organized citizen tax revolts such as California's Proposition 13 and Massachusetts's Proposition 2 ½ have constrained public spending in many parts of the country; less formal resistance and campaigns for privatization have carried the day in others. Continued competition between states and localities to attract capital investment has in part been played out through efforts to reduce tax burdens, either for all taxpayers or for business. They have decreased revenue while sometimes imposing new costs for amenities to attract business.

Despite these conditions, communities have found ways to generate income for new initiatives. Some have also managed to shift assets into the social and public domain in an era when the reverse—pushing more of them into the private sector—has been considered efficient and wise.

Privatization has been a familiar theme in the 1980s, both in the United States and abroad. Forms of social ownership have rarely been achieved in conjunction with more thoroughgoing transformation of

---

found in Robin Murray, "Ownership, Control, and the Market," *New Left Review* No. 164 (July–August 1987), 87–112. Detailed discussion of activities of the Greater London Council and the Greater London Enterprise Board is presented in Maureen Mackintosh and Hilary Wainwright, eds., *A Taste of Power: The Politics of Local Economics* (London, 1987). See also John Gyford, *The Politics of Local Socialism* (London, 1985). Historical material on the U.S. experience with socialist administrations in cities such as Milwaukee, Schenectady, New York., and Bridgeport, Connecticut, is presented in Bruce M. Stave, ed., *Socialism and the Cities* (Port Washington, N.Y., 1975).

[2] See Gar Alperovitz and Jeff Faux, *Rebuilding America* (New York, 1984), and Carnoy and Shearer, *Economic Democracy,* chap. 2, for discussion of larger-scale public enterprise in the United States. Analysis of the problems of controlling public agencies such as the Tennessee Valley Authority and Port Authority of New York/New Jersey can be found in Annmarie Hauck Walsh, *The Public's Business* (Cambridge, Mass., 1978).

social relations of production or use. We will return to that issue in Chapter 7. Here we present recent examples of public asset creation in the United States and investigate the funding of these projects through existing local and national tax systems.

Local Public Land

Boulder, Colorado, is not a poor community. Many residents have had both income enough and environmental awareness enough to make protection of the city's setting on the eastern slopes of the Rocky Mountains a high priority. Development pressure threatened open space within the city as well as around it. Residents took action on both fronts; they did so before many other communities did and more aggressively.

Federal action at the turn of the century had secured mountain territory near Boulder as parkland, and local public initiative created an adjacent seventy-five–acre Chautauqua that became the home of the Colorado Music Festival. In the late 1950s and early 1960s, local environmentalists blocked development on mesas surrounding the city by an amendment to the city's charter, declaring the development not in its best interest and making city water for it unavailable. That success was the basis for formalizing an organization to safeguard greenspace in the city and county; PLAN (People's League for Action Now)-Boulder was the result. PLAN-Boulder became active in local politics, encouraging environmentalists to run for city council and endorsing candidates who were in tune with its objectives. It organized a major conference on greenbelts, and held regular luncheon meetings open to all residents. According to one long-time member, residents viewed the organization as powerful and responsible; when asked to speak before its meetings, local officials or planners generally responded favorably, establishing opportunities for creative discussion.[3]

The stopgap charter amendment was devised to buy land that would remain undeveloped, including expansion of the city-county greenbelt system. A funding mechanism to eliminate bond-issue referendums for each acquisition was foreseen. In 1967, city voters approved a

[3] Summary is from Josephine Robertson, ed., "Highlights of PLAN-Boulder County 1959–1986," photocopy (n.d.); "Remarks of Bob McKelvey at the annual dinner meeting of PLAN-Boulder County, January 25, 1987," photocopy; and interview with Janet Roberts, a founding member of PLAN-Boulder, Boulder, Colorado, July 15, 1987.

dedicated, one-cent addition to the sales tax. Forty percent of it would go to acquisition of open land, and 60 percent to road improvements. The fund, which is supervised by the Open Space Board of Trustees appointed by the city government, now generates close to $5 million a year for open-land acquisition. Income from the dedicated sales tax serves as a basis for increasing the bonding capacity for land acquisition, and by 1986 over twenty thousand acres had been permanently brought under administration of the Open Space Board. That land consists of city parks, mountain parks, and open space, much of it in the county surrounding the city.

Boulder's commitment to open greenspace extends into the heart of the city as well. Boulder Creek flows out of the mountains and through the center of town. Land on its banks forms a strip park that provides walking and bicycle paths, fishing sites, and a natural link to the foothills. It also acts as a crucial flood control area.

PLAN-Boulder was active early enough to affect Boulder County's planning as well. A joint city-county planning effort resulted in the 1970 Boulder Valley Comprehensive Plan, and more than two hundred and fifty community meetings helped shape a county-wide plan enacted in 1978.[4] The plan has helped to control growth in unincorporated parts of the county by such means as preserving agricultural land-use areas, particularly in the fast-developing Boulder-Denver corridor. The county has contributed to acquisition of open space through general revenues, but several attempts to implement a dedicated portion of the county sales tax for land acquistion have failed.

Boulder's strong stance on environmental, quality-of-life, and open-space issues has not gone untested. Although the University of Colorado helps maintain the economy on a more even keel than many of the region's other cities, Boulder has lost thousands of manufacturing jobs over the past decade. Its favorable setting and location near Denver have attracted potential employers, but their impact has not always been welcomed. Systems Development Corporation, for instance, wanted to locate a plant on the southern edge of the city which was expected to employ four thousand people. Boulder rejected

[4] Interview with Josie Heath, Boulder County Commissioner, Boulder, Colorado, July 15, 1987. Land-use plans are delineated in "Boulder County Comprehensive Plan: Goals, Policies and Maps," Boulder County Planning Commission, April 1978, with revisions December 1986; and the Boulder Valley Comprehensive Plan, City of Boulder Planning Department and Boulder County Land Use Department, revised through October 9, 1986.

the company's request to rezone agricultural land counted as greenbelt and offered the company an alternate location.[5] Systems Development moved to Virginia instead. Industrial jobs remain at a premium in Boulder.

PLAN-Boulder has taken positive action on other development issues. It was a strong supporter of the extensive bikeway system and joined with other citizens' groups to promote the Urban Renewal Authority for purposes of locating a large regional shopping center inside the city limits rather than on its perimeter. The authority assembled land for the project, and a number of citizens' groups worked with the city and the developer on siting and design. The mall gives privileged access to pedestrians, bicycles, and public transportation; contains community meeting and child-care space; and has extensive landscaping and trees in parking areas. It also, of course, contributes sales-tax revenue to the city.

Boulder does not have the feel of a city of eighty-five thousand residents because other constraints on growth have helped retain the physical quality of life of a unique, smaller place. Building height is limited to fifty-five feet, thirty-five feet in its Victorian historic district, which also contains a successful pedestrian mall. A 2 percent annual growth limitation is controlled by restricting building permits in a process that gives preferential treatment to multi-family housing.[6] All housing development is subject to a 15 percent moderate- and low-income requirement.

Boulder's land acquisition does not bring an income-producing asset under public control. Some of the acquired land is parkland that must be maintained, and although maintenance does generate local jobs, it is an expense in the city budget. This land is available for use, however, by residents rich and poor, and it helps sustain quality of life across generations. On the other hand the land acquisition has been financed through a sales tax, a regressive form of taxation that will be discussed later in this chapter. While falling disproportionately on lower income residents, the sales tax has extracted revenue from

[5] Iver Peterson, "Economic Glow Fading beside Majestic Rockies," *New York Times*, December 28, 1985, and "Highlights of PLAN-Boulder County," pp. 27–30.

[6] Removing acreage from the pool of both developable land and restrictive zoning serves to push housing prices up. Boulder has had to take action to assure a sufficient supply of reasonably priced housing for its working population.

a transient population of students who benefit from use of Boulder's parks.

Income-Generating Local Assets

Taxation is linked to the continual appeal from the public sector for funds to create and maintain infrastructure and to deliver services. Dedicated tax revenues, special fees, the borrowing power of governments, and other funding sources can be used more aggressively to acquire assets that bring with them a new stream of income.

The key element of many development projects has been the sale of public land to private developers. The land may have come into the public domain because of tax foreclosure, or perhaps a municipality assembled parcels in order to facilitate a development deal. By sale of the land to the private sector, it is returned to the city's tax base, where it generates an annual stream of income. The municipality gets a part of the income stream associated with the property, as well as the sale price. But should the public entity necessarily step aside?

Consider Santa Monica, California. Its municipal airport serves much of the general aviation in the West Los Angeles basin. Corporate and private jets of the rich and famous call this airport home. In aerial photos of densely populated West Los Angeles–Santa Monica–Beverley Hills, the airport stands out as one of the last parcels of relatively open land. The City of Santa Monica recognized that it was underutilized space: The airport's hangar and maintenance facilities were scattered over both sides of its runway. When the buildings were consolidated on one side, thirty-seven and a half acres of land became available. Rather than sell it off, the city formulated plans for its development which could not only mean an increasing stream of income to the city, but its right to appreciation in value in a land-scarce urban area as well.

Santa Monica worked with a developer who would build and run office, child-care, and office support services on the city's land. Long-term leases were expected to generate $4–5 million per year in ground rent revenue, and participation in other revenues generated by activities on the site could have eventually dwarfed that figure.[7] The city

[7] From planning data of the Office of Community and Economic Development, City of Santa Monica, and interview with Peggy Curran, director, OCED, March 20, 1989.

would have maintained greater control over the nature and scale of the development than it might have through land-use regulation alone, and it could share in the resulting cash flow. This form of ownership has its advantages. Opposition to additional growth in the area halted the project, and what use will be made of this land is unclear.

Shopping mall development has also felt the influence of expanding public entrepreneurship. A town, county, or city more commonly will assemble a land parcel and use it to assure itself not only a voice but also an equity position in the development. That role can net the public entity rights to a significant percentage of the net cash flow generated by mall merchants' rental payments. It also increases the public entity's ability to locate malls in ways that are consistent with its land-use plans, rather than having to fight unwelcome private initiatives.

Urban developments are demonstrating a variety of similar public-private partnerships that yield new public funds. For instance, San Antonio and Cincinnati are both engaged in downtown hotel projects that assure them a portion of revenues. In both cases, their involvement was linked to attracting hotel facilities that were deemed essential to downtown revitalization. Cincinnati also participated in the construction of a headquarters building for one of its banks.[8]

Recent entrepreneurial activity in California has been spurred on by a quest for new revenue sources for local governments in the wake of Proposition 13. However, initiatives of this kind have a longer history grounded in broader goals. Planning for the Hartford, Connecticut, Civic Center began in the 1960s amid considerable debate over the level of public funding it should entail, what form any public-private partnership should take, and the amount of money that could be raised for it from area businesses. By late 1970 Hartford's City Council had specified a goal of retaining title to Civic Center land and controlling its operation through leases.[9] By the time the project was launched, city residents had agreed to a $30 million bond issue. A hotel on the site payed a fee to the city in lieu of taxes, with a long-term lease that eventually returned it to the city. Space over the complex was leased to developers on the basis of air rights. In addition

[8] Lawrence M. Fisher, "Cities Turn into Entrepreneurs," *New York Times*, April 4, 1987.

[9] See Pierre Clavel, *The Progressive City: Planning and Participation 1969–1984* (New Brunswick, N.J., 1986), chap. 2, for a discussion of Hartford's governance in the decade of 1969–79. See pp. 30–36 for information on the Civic Center and other real estate transactions.

to regular lease fees, the city claimed 1 percent of gross rental rates collected by the developer.

Income for Hartford was not the only concern on the minds of progressive council members. City ownership and lease arrangements allowed them to stipulate that part-time jobs in the Civic Center would go to students in the city's high schools as part of work-study arrangements, that a specified percentage of residents and minorities would be part of the hotel's union staff and various construction contracts, and that minority businesses would get some of those contracts. Nicholas Carbone, the person responsible for structuring the Civic Center deal, sketched the following development strategy. Hartford, like many cities, had lost jobs and much of its middle class. It had vacant and underutilized land and a poor population that needed jobs. The task was to convert land into jobs. If that was accomplished, there would be a resource base from which city services could be improved. In addition, land acquired by the city for its citizens would appreciate and generate higher revenues. This strategy, along with tax abatements to help bring about other needed development, was aimed at placing Hartford in a stronger competitive position for new investment relative to its suburban perimeter.[10] Hartford's entrepreneurial activity remained wedded to the common urban redevelopment strategy of attempting to make the center city attractive again for those who have fled to the suburbs.

The tradition of public entrepreneur/developer also exists in the form of development corporations, such as the New York/New Jersey Port Authority and the New York City Public Development Corporation. The Port Authority operates in multiple counties and two states around the New York metropolitan area and develops public infrastructure in addition to owning and managing extensive real estate. The New York City Public Development Corporation is a municipally based nonprofit corporation. Formed in 1966, it has a large staff of planners, engineers, and attorneys who work with developers on large projects such as a Brooklyn office building for the investment bank Morgan Stanley. The city invested $12 million of its funds in the $130 million project, and it gets 25 percent of the building's net cash flow.[11] Both of these corporations have been strongly criticized for abuses of power, lack of cooperation with regulatory agencies, and lack of

[10] Ibid., p. 32.
[11] Fisher, "Cities Turn into Entrepreneurs."

concern for the impact of some projects on area residents. They serve as a reminder that private, for-profit organizations have no monopoly on arrogance. New models are badly needed for structuring development corporations for more complete, ongoing public supervision and control.

Can initiatives of this kind be held accountable to the communities they are created to serve? To help assure that outcome, they should first implement public plans. Their work must be evaluated in light of clearly articulated goals that derive from open, participatory governance. Second, their internal processes and decision making should fall under the review of publicly constituted boards of directors. Confidentiality may be necessary for specific negotiation and dealmaking, but public accountability and oversight are essential.

Public entrepreneurship carries with it risks and problems. Risks of the marketplace are inherent. A project that promises a portion of profit may never generate any. Rental streams can be adversely affected by later developments or macroeconomic downturns. Problems can arise when public officials get caught up in "doing deals" with public money and fail to do the careful analyses and prudent planning essential to assure positive outcomes for these projects. Dealmaking also can provide local leaders with excuses for secret negotiations that stifle public participation, and at worst they raise additional possibilities for inside deals, bribes, and kickbacks. Administrations that engage in them must possess sound financial, legal, and negotiating skills and be "squeaky clean."

Municipal Utilities

States and municipalities deliver a variety of basic services for two reasons. One is uninterrupted operation of essential services. A city government is unlikely to decide to get out of the business of delivering water or sewer services to its residents. The other is that private, for-profit corporations cannot make a profit running these services unless, of course, they are allowed to exploit a monopoly position. Few governments could allow private firms to do that for long, so they turn to what are often called public utilities.

Public utilities, however, are not always what they appear to be. If they are publicly regulated private firms, they are given monopoly rights to deliver services in an area, but their operation comes under the supervision of federal, state, or local watchdog agencies that are supposed to keep both their levels of service and pricing in line. Under these arrangements private utility providers return the best possible level of profit they can to their stockholders, and regulators try to restrict their net income to a level just high enough to attract investment. The profit rate is lower than in many other industries because the monopoly position in their market area and the regulatory agency's ability to adjust prices diminish risk and uncertainty for the investor. The rationale for a utility's monopoly is economies of scale in operation; the per unit cost of electrical generation and transmission diminishes up to some point at a large scale of operation. Thus, if price is controlled to drive out monopoly profits, consumers should pay the lowest price possible. That is the theory.

In practice, this system too can break down. Regulatory agencies are staffed with industry insiders because they have expert knowledge. They may also have the best interest of industry owners and managers at heart and only secondary concern for consumers. The firms themselves may behave as if growth in demand for their product was their primary objective, rather than recognizing the competing rationales of low price or conservation.

Massena Electric Department

Concerned that regulation of utilities was inadequate and experiencing dramatic price increases, some communities have taken bold action. The City of Massena, New York, had discussed the feasiblity of establishing its own electric power company in the 1960s.[12] Its favorable location near generating facilities on the St. Lawrence River and the example of other cities in the state with municipal power encouraged its idea of breaking away from the Niagara Mohawk Power Corporation, its privately owned, regional utility company. Faced with rising oil costs and costs for nuclear plants in the 1970s, Niagara Mohawk raised prices rapidly. Massena began talking municipal power again. The city commissioned a feasability study in early 1974, which recommended that the city make an offer to purchase its local distribution system from Niagara Mohawk. A bipartisan citizens' committee recommended approval, and the area United

[12] The following discussion is from Vic Reinemer, "Why Massena Wins," *Public Power*, September-October 1986, 10–15; Massena Electric Department, 1987 and 1989 *Progress Reports*; and telephone interview with Clifford G. Engstrom, superintendent, Massena Electric Department, December 6, 1988.

Auto Workers local put up $2,500 (the only money used to promote approval). Niagara Mohawk spent $290,000 campaigning against it, but that was money down the drain. Over 60 percent of Massena residents voted for local public power.

Massena's battle had just begun. Its $2.8 million offer to Niagara Mohawk was rejected. Over the next seven years the city pursued legal routes to overcome Niagara Mohawk's refusal to deliver power to Massena even if the city did own its distribution system. By 1980 Niagara Mohawk was indicating a willingness to sell, but at a far higher price; in 1981 the combatants settled for $7.7 million. The purchase price, legal fees, and initial operating funds required a $10.5 million bond issue, which residents approved by a wide margin.

The Massena Electric Department is run as a separate entity in the city government. Its appointed Electric Utility Board serves staggered, unpaid terms, and it sets policy. The superintendent manages the system. Work rules for employees are spelled out in contracts with the International Brotherhood of Electrical Workers.

This carefully planned take-over had promised consumers a 20 percent rate cut and continuation of local tax payments at the same rate that Niagara Mohawk had been paying on its facilities. Both promises were kept. In a 1989 report, the Electric Department proudly pointed to eight and a half years of operation without a rate increase. In 1987 its rates were 40 percent below Niagara Mohawk's in the surrounding area of upstate New York. After winning the right to purchase additional Niagara preference hydropower in 1989, this system was able to lower its rates by 20 percent. By late 1989, its rates were half those of Niagara Mohawk. Substantial capital improvements have been made, including a bond-financed substation that replaced two older, less efficient substations.

Based on rates charged by Niagara Mohawk, the transition was estimated to have saved area residents and businesses $14 million, well over its purchase costs, in its first six and a half years of operation. Much of that money was no doubt spent in the community, with beneficial multiplier effects. Substantially less money has been flowing out of the community to pay large legal and public relations expenses, high executive salaries, and stockholder dividends at Niagara Mohawk. Residents paid a high price to break from the secure world of a regulated private utility provider, but they found they could save even more and gain more control over delivery of this service in their community.

Massena's public electric system is well known in New York state because of the protracted battle to establish it. It is considered unique because of its close proximity to a major hydropower facility, but in fact it buys its power out of a state-supervised grid, just as other municipal power companies and large corporate users do. More surprising is that it is one of fifty municipal operations in New York. Some were begun as municipal systems at the turn of the century; others were created during the Depression. They tend to be isolated pockets of local control and lower cost within the vast territories of the state's several publicly regulated, privately owned utility companies.[13]

The Massena case is a reminder that the basic economic principles underlying large-scale, regulated public utilities may have to be rethought, or at least applied more carefully. Economies of scale in generating power can be attained by individual projects of large firms, or by regional and even international projects entered into by consortia of smaller firms. Massena's example indicates that economies of scale may still apply in the generation of electric power (alternative power sources aside), but those same economies may not result in distribution of the power. Municipal systems can therefore be compatible with confederate development and maintenance of large-scale generating facilities and transmission lines.

We can only guess that Niagara Mohawk's resistance to losing Massena, a very small part of its market, was based on concern for the precedent it would set and the demonstration effect it could have for other communities. Since it would diminish growth in demand, it could also be seen as a threat to rates elsewhere and ultimately to the utility's financial return to its stockholders. Again, the need to maintain a sufficient level of private appropriation of social surplus can sell most citizens short.

Taxes and Local Public Assets

Each of the local public assets described in this chapter has been created with use of public funds. Each enhances the well-being of

[13] Municipal systems exist throughout the country. They do not have an unblemished record, but some are undergoing considerable reform. See Peter Asmus, "Sacramento Utility Wired for Change," *In These Times*, March 14–20, 1990, 9. Recently they have been more responsive in implementing meaningful conservation programs than many private utilities have been. See David Moberg, "Electric Companies See Utility of Blackmail," *In These Times*, December 20, 1989–January 9, 1990, 7.

community residents, whether by assuring open vistas and space for recreation, by expanding the stream of income to public coffers and a public voice in development planning and management, or by cutting the cost of a basic need and increasing local control over the conditions of its provision. Assets of this kind must be acquired. Public debt plays a prominent role in their acquisition, but borrowing is made possible by the community's regular income in the form of tax revenue. Taxes and tax reform are subjects in need of new and critical thinking, as well as more progressive practical outcomes. The following is a discussion of some of the most fundamental issues and their relation to local public initiatives.

A very real source of frustration with local taxes is that they have risen, in real terms, in a period of stagnant or declining real income.[14] People feel poorer because they are, and they resent the bills that arrive demanding more taxes for services that they take for granted or that they feel can be dispensed with, given their other needs and wants.

Local income tax is often restricted by state law, and when used it is generally proportional. New York City is a notable exception with a progressive local income tax.[15] Local taxes commonly take two basic forms: sales taxes and property taxes. Sales taxes are regressive. They are borne by consumers in proportion to their total expenditures, and as income goes up the proportion of income used for consumption diminishes. They can be made somewhat less regressive by excluding essentials such as food, clothing, and medical supplies.

Property taxes are ambiguous in intent, but generally regressive in outcome. To the extent that they are a tax on wealth held in the form of real property, they are progressive. But to the extent that people's residences are necessary to their lives, this form of taxation can be seen as regressive.[16] Landlords usually pass on to tenants taxes on

[14] This point was made by Randy Albelda in "A Progressive Tax Agenda for the 1990s," a presentation at the summer conference of the Union for Radical Political Economics, Sandwich, Massachusetts, August 25, 1989. State and local income and sales tax rates increased in the period of 1966–85, whereas property tax rates declined. State and local taxes in that period together accounted for a gradually rising share of gross national product, stabilizing in the 1980s at 11 to 12 percent of GNP. See Joseph A. Pechman, *Who Paid the Taxes, 1966–85* (Washington, D.C., 1985), p. 65. For additional data on the 1980s, see *Economic Report of the President* (Washington, D.C., 1988), pp. 250–51.

[15] See Donald Phares, *Who Pays State and Local Taxes?* (Cambridge, Mass., 1980), pp. 101–2.

[16] For several articles that deal with the relationship between property taxes and the

rental housing, which makes the taxes regressive. For low-income homeowners, one progressive reform takes the form of a "circuit-breaker" provision that limits the percentage of income an owner pays in property tax.

At the level of states, income tax becomes the central issue. This form of tax has been adopted by all but a few states. State income tax rates have been proportional or mildly progressive. Making them more progressive would provide funds to assist poorer communities through redistribution in the state. An important example is the funding of education, now heavily dependent on local property taxes. Resources for education are meager in poorer communities and more readily available in communities with substantial property values. Revenue from more progressive state income tax could be used to eliminate this inequity.

Rather than boost income taxes across the board or make them more progressive, states have rushed to enact lotteries, "voluntary taxes" whose incidence falls heavily on the poor.[17] State sales taxes could be made less regressive in the same way as sales taxes at the local level by eliminating them on items generally deemed necessities of life. More fundamentally, both lotteries and state sales taxes could be replaced by more progressive state income tax systems.

The logic of these proposals is a simple and enduring principle of American life: Taxes should be assessed fairly. Defining the term "fair" is less simple. At minimum, it must mean eliminating regressive taxes at local, state, and national levels. In our view, it means making taxes progressive whenever possible, so that they take proportionately more from those who have been favored by the working of the system.

The Limit to Local Taxation

This chapter points to several ways in which communities have managed to build new public assets in a period of "fiscal austerity." These are, to us, positive examples of communities bringing more social surplus under democratic control, where it stands a greater chance of being put to work based on democratically made choices

---

nation's housing problems see Bratt, Hartman, and Meyerson, eds., *Critical Perspectives on Housing.*

[17] Charles T. Clotfelter and Phillip J. Cook, *Selling Hope: State Lotteries in America* (Cambridge, Mass., 1989).

and of being used for the public good. Having said that, we now must place this form of local initiative in a more critical context. The way in which these projects are financed at the local level is regressive, and ultimately it must be changed. For reasons just mentioned, that change cannot be accomplished solely at the local level.

Progressive taxation at the local level encounters a familiar response from capital. Raise capital's tax burden, and it may move elsewhere. This response works against community action on taxes in the same way that it works against labor demands for better wages or working conditions. The solution is to use federal law to establish uniform basic rules for taxation and spending and to return a large portion of federal tax revenue to local public control after it is collected.

Federal taxation also has its progressive and regressive components. Progressivity has been eroded in income taxes for both individuals and corporations. Both tax structures were more steeply progressive in the heyday of mid-twentieth–century capitalism, and arguments that they should be made less progressive in order that our economy can function more efficiently are highly suspect. In other areas of federal taxation, estate taxes could be a more significant source of revenue without undermining the will to accumulate. Payroll taxes are generally borne by employees, even when paid by employers.[18] Funding for the social security system could be made less regressive by lifting the income cap on payments, and perhaps then lowering rates for everyone.

Transfer payments are a means of achieving redistribution from those with significant income to those without it. They have gained a bad reputation in recent years, and they deserve it to the extent that they are carried out through a demeaning system of government handouts. However, what their opponents often resent is that they are very progressive means of redistribution. Recast as a way of entitling all members of society to the basic needs of life, and administered in a more community-based, decentralized way, transfers can be an important tool in redressing the growing disparities in the original dis-

[18] Federal income tax rates and their overall incidence remained progressive in the mid-1980s, although they were less so than in the previous two decades. The impact of rising payroll taxes (regressive) and declining corporate taxes (generally assumed to be progressive) meant that federal taxes became less progressive in this period. Pechman, *Who Paid the Taxes,* chaps. 1, 3, 5, and esp. p. 31. For other sources of federal taxation see the discussion in Richard A. Musgrave and Peggy B. Musgrave, *Public Finance in Theory and Practice*, 4th ed. (New York, 1984).

tribution of income from our market economy.[19] They are a reform with positive, material results.

The tax burden Americans face is low compared to that of other Western industrial nations, and through much of the 1980s a growing portion of what we did pay in taxes was devoted to the wasteful expansion of military spending.[20] Our combined tax burden from local, state, and federal taxes has little or no impact on the exaggerated spread of incomes in this country. The bill for high-income and wealthy Americans' tax holiday is coming due. As a nation we face the challenge of rebuilding transportation infrastructure, improving the health and education of a large percentage of citizens, cleaning up our past waste, and safeguarding the environment. Much of this is work to be done at the local level, but the resources needed to do it must be drawn by a progressive, uniform national tax system. Future political struggles will determine who will pay the bill. From our perspective, they provide opportunity to define a larger portion of social surplus as public and to redirect a much larger portion of that surplus to local control.

[19] Pechman, *Who Paid the Taxes,* pp. 51–52, 60–61, 44–52. *Business Week* Magazine and Standard & Poor's Compustat Services provide one indicator of this rising disparity in their comparison of compensation in various occupations over time. For example, in 1960 a corporate chief executive officer's before-tax pay was thirty-eight times that of a teacher in this country. In 1988 his or her take-home pay was seventy-two times that of a teacher. Progressive taxation reduced the multiple for take-home pay from 38 to 11 in 1960. In 1988 a less progressive tax system reduced the multiple from 72 to 66. See Leonard Silk, "Economic Scene," *New York Times*, May 12, 1989.

[20] By official measure, recognized by many observers as excluding several defense-related costs, Reagan-era "military Keynesianism" pushed defense spending up from 23.6 to 27.9 percent of federal outlays from fiscal year 1981 to fiscal year 1986. In constant (1982) dollars, the six years marked an increase in defense spending of 41 percent. See U.S. Bureau of the Census, *Statistical Abstract 1988*, p. 294.

7

Collective Action, Communities, and Social Change

Based on our sense that much of the economic analysis of community development lacks sufficiently radical insight,[1] we have devoted most of our energy to encouraging rethinking in that area. Development, however, is an integrated process, and we turn here to some of its less economistic aspects, to issues associated with expanding the practice of democracy, the nature of collective action, and the relationship between local and national political activity.

Expanding democracy will require continuation of the struggles of working people, minority groups, women, and others who have been excluded from full participation in the past. Realistic goals include, but are not limited to, (1) developing for all citizens the right and ability to play active roles in shaping the public decisions that affect their lives and (2) bringing more fully under democratic control an increasing percentage of the institutions in which we function. Effective democracy is based on the need for certain forms of equality in practice. They include not only equal voting rights, but also equal access to education, lawmakers, and public officials, equality of voice in public matters including access to communications media, and general equality of time and resources with which to engage in public activities. Extremes of inequality in income and wealth—particularly in the ability to live on income from property—undermine "equal access." Dramatic differences in educational opportunity do as well,

[1] Radical in the sense of going to the root.

and they are, of course, linked closely to the distribution of income and wealth.[2]

Expanding democratic control over the institutions of society is fundamentally hampered by capitalism. Most adults spend a third of their day working in organizations that limit rights to participation and truncate civil liberties as conditions of employment. Institutions of business are privately owned and controlled, and they are, therefore, subject to democratic control only in the very distant imposition of sanctions for unlawful action. Most of the people who work in these enterprises do not control them or run them. Principles of democracy do not apply. Neither do they apply in determining investment location or deciding whether investment will take place at all. Joshua Cohen and Joel Rogers get to the heart of the matter when they argue that investment "is effectively the only guarantee of a society's future. If that future is not available as a subject of social deliberation, then social deliberations are fundamentally constrained and incomplete."[3] The goal, after all, is to change the way in which we produce so that surplus is appropriated and put to use by and for all of society, not one class.

The practice of democracy is also limited and skewed by capitalism in our nonwork lives as citizens and consumers.[4] Our primary concern remains development in the broadest sense. From that perspective, we derive the following three observations.

1. Capitalist market economies, even in their mixed and constrained

[2] See Christopher Jencks et al., *Inequality: A Reassessment of the Effect of Family and Schooling in America* (New York, 1972), and Samuel Bowles and Herbert Gintis, *Schooling in Capitalist America* (New York, 1976).

[3] Joshua Cohen and Joel Rogers, *On Democracy: Toward a Transformation of American Society* (New York, 1983), p. 161. For an analysis of how organizations of work can be structured democratically and the barriers to achieving that goal under current conditions in the United States, see Gunn, *Workers' Self-Management,* and Greenberg, *Workplace Democracy.*

[4] Some important contributions to a growing literature on this issue are Benjamin Barber, *Strong Democracy: Participatory Politics for a New Age* (Berkeley, Calif., 1984); Bowles and Gintis, *Democracy and Capitalism: Property, Community, and the Contradictions of Modern Social Thought* (New York, 1986); Cohen and Rogers, *On Democracy*; Robert A. Dahl, *Democracy and Its Critics* (New Haven, Conn., 1989); Sheldon Wolin, *The Presence of the Past* (Baltimore, Md., 1989). Important lessons from feminist thought and practice need to be added to this work. See Barrett, *Women's Oppression Today,* and Sheila Rowbotham, Lynne Segal, and Hilary Wainwright, *Beyond the Fragments: Feminism and the Making of Socialism* (London, 1979). A very practical application of feminist experience to the practice of democracy is illustrated in Hilary Wainwright, "New Forms of Democracy for Socialist Renewal," *Socialist Review* 20 (April–June 1990), 31–44.

forms, bias their societies to belittle or ignore the "social self." They cause us to forget or neglect the ways in which our lives as citizens, producers, consumers, and learners are *social.*[5] In the most virulent of free-market economic ideology, conscious political pursuit of public goods by "private" actors is destructive of private rights and values and is illegitimate. Even in more liberal formulations, there exists a poverty of conceptual recognition of the empathy that forms the basis of collective action. Ben Barber describes market-based "economic man" as devoid of imagination and argues forcefully that it is imagination that makes possible "common will[ing] and the creation of political communities."[6]

2. Capitalism perverts the public sphere to private economic ends. The commercialization of life, the difficulty of earning a living, and the lack of public discourse over the real conditions of life mean that public action is limited to tinkering with a market economic. Political struggle centers on issues such as welfare policies or the level of the minimum wage. Capitalist conceptions of efficiency are accepted as fundamental, as is the goal of economic growth. Gains in social justice that can be won through political struggle under these conditions are generally accompanied by the onus of consent to the system.[7] Politics is co-opted into a contest, on uneven terrain, for short-term material gain. Mirroring the private and exclusionary world of economic activity, political engagement becomes divisive: men against women, skilled workers against less skilled, whites against people of color. Politics in the full sense of the term is impossible.

3. Finally and perhaps most obvious, the very essence of the cherished idea of liberty is undercut by the concentration of private power in accumulated capital. Individual choice and democratic accountability are central to meaningful democracy; they are mostly absent in conditions of work in the modern corporation, in the lack of accountability enjoyed by capital, and in capital's ability to use the state—itself heavily insulated from democratic control—to serve its ends.[8] The modern corporation is not alone in its corrosively unde-

[5] Bowles and Gintis, *Democracy and Capitalism.*

[6] Barber, *Strong Democracy,* pp. 254–55. To be gender neutral, Barber's description should have included women, although they seem to have been less afflicted by this condition than have men.

[7] Cohen and Rogers, *On Democracy,* p. 146.

[8] By the term "the state," we mean to invoke not the individual state in the republic, but the institutions of governance, socialization, and control at the broadest political, social, and geographic levels.

mocratic impact on society; the patriarchal family and educational institutions, among others, are similarly undemocratic and deserving of radical transformation. Their democracy-warping power is partly economic, but none is so central to the economic system as is today's corporate institutional home for accumulated capital.

Overcoming these barriers requires revitalization of what is commonly described as the country's impoverished public life. The most often cited indicator of its malaise is voter participation rates of approximately half of eligible voters in national elections and a third in many state and local contests.[9] Even though these figures address only a small part of a citizen's role in a democracy, voting is for most people their primary form of participation in governance. Yet a variety of contemporary observers of American society persuasively argue the existence of latent potential for renewed political engagement. People take part in a wide variety of voluntary organizations and are increasingly drawn to issue-based social movements. The authors of *Habits of the Heart* urge renewed commitment in the civic republican tradition. Others see renewal linked to the economic mid-level, and now increasingly middle-aged, baby-boom generation because of its desire for more meaningful political participation. Alternately, Harry Boyte points to a potential "backyard revolution," resulting from a rebirth of democratic community values, a process of empowerment, and the rise of a new populism.[10] Despite their merits, each of these important arguments is limited by its separation from a clear analysis of economic reality and by the ways that capitalism itself stifles the expansion of public life. With the exception of Boyte, consent to the

[9] See Walter D. Burnham, *The Current Crisis in American Politics* (New York, 1982), chaps. 4 and 5, and "The 1980 Earthquake: Realignment, Reaction or What?" in *The Hidden Election: Politics and Economics in the 1980 Presidential Campaign,* Thomas Ferguson and Joel Rogers, eds. (New York, 1981). Historical analysis of this phenomenon is contained in Burnham, "The Appearance and Disappearance of the American Voter," in *The Political Economy,* Ferguson and Rogers, eds. (Armonk, N.Y., 1984), pp. 112–39. On the limited nature of the franchise, see Barber, *Strong Democracy*, pp. 145 and 187–88. Barber likens voting to "using a public toilet," where we "wait in line with a crowd in order to close ourselves up in a small compartment where we can relieve ourselves in solitude..." (p. 188).

[10] Robert N. Bellah et al., *Habits of the Heart: Individualism and Commitment in American Life* (Berkeley, Calif., 1985). An example of renewal linked to the baby-boom generation can be found in the description of the "new collar Americans" in Ralph Whitehead, Jr., "New Collar America: An Overview," background paper for a speech before the Democratic Policy Committee, Washington, D.C., July 10, 1985. For the "backyard revolution" see Harry C. Boyte, *Backyard Revolution: Understanding the New Citizen Movement* (Philadelphia, 1980), and *Community Is Possible.*

system has also limited the analytical insight to be gained by much of this literature.

The term "community" carries with it attractive connotations of decentralization in governance. Decisions that affect people's lives take place at all levels of government, but at the local level most citizens have the greatest opportunity to be directly involved in making them. There they have the greatest access to elected and appointed officials and to public records and information. There they also deal face-to-face with other citizens concerned with the process and its outcomes.

We have argued for encouraging these attributes by raising the economic content of local democratic decision making. Below is a summary of the potential positive outcomes of local action to bring more social surplus under community control. This summary reaches back into the work of the preceding chapters and propels us forward into questions about the ability of local action to further new, more progressive directions of change.

—Planning for change, public stewardship, and management of real resources engage people. This expanded public activity can help foster thinking and debate over the merits of new proposals and forms of their implementation. The diversity of various communities' approaches to solving problems and creating new opportunities can enrich public life.

—Opening and expanding public forums can help shift the focus of political discourse to ordinary people and their problems and aspirations. In national political campaigns of the 1980s, Jesse Jackson had the ability to bring local issues, from farm foreclosures to neighborhood "crack houses," into the national political arena. He made a point of being in touch with ordinary citizens. The next step is to have more citizens engaged in the process.

—Attempts to plan at the local level, and to sustain community economic development, can educate concerned citizens about the powers they must confront. Analysis of a local economy often lays bare the dependency of the economy on a few institutions and the linkages those institutions have to distant decision makers. Knowledge of the flow of funds into and out of the community allows more cleareyed bargaining with both local and transnational capital. One result can be a better understanding of the impact of international conditions of workers, women, minorities, and the environment on the local community.

—Community-based activity teaches the skills necessary to become engaged citizens, leaders, coordinators, and analysts. Skills developed in one area of activity, such as organizing shelters for battered women, are basically those needed to take on other work, such as winning improvements in public transportation. Labor union locals have historically served as training grounds for full-time and occasional organizers. Although many continue to do so, others could be revitalized by skills learned from women and men who have been active in other community-based work. Techniques and skills developed during the civil rights movement have continuing significance for many aspects of community development; gay and lesbian activists and others have benefited from its lessons.

—Community-based work is not unidimensional. Bringing to the fore issues of gender, race, and class reminds us that regional and national political activity too will require the hard work of forming linkages, compromise, and sharing of burdens and opportunities. A progressive political resurgence in the United States will probably not arise from one movement. But a broader, shared vision of a more democratic and egalitarian future is the glue that is essential for linkages among movements and more traditional progressive political forces such as organized labor. At the local level particularly, in grassroots community organizing, labor is redefining a vital role for itself.[11]

Can communities organize to define a broader field of action than they have traditionally pursued? We have argued that they can but that in order to do so they must become more assertive in redefining their relationship with capital. Given a social and political vision matched by some greater degree of unity and will, they can begin to redefine the process of development itself.

Collective Action

Two types of local collective action are particularly relevant to creating new forms of development. One can be labeled resistance to

[11] See Jeremy Brecher and Tim Costello, "Community Labor Coalitions," *Z Magazine,* April 1990, pp. 79–85, and their extensive collection of articles on this topic in Brecher and Costello, *Building Bridges: The Emerging Grassroots Coalition of Labor and Community* (New York, 1990). The world of ideas and culture is an important part of this process as well. See Norman Birnbaum, *The Radical Renewal: The Politics of Ideas in Modern America* (New York, 1988).

capital, which is characterized by efforts, some successful and some not, to block implementation of the private investment process. Examples include numerous attempts to stop shopping malls, to block large projects such as the Coliseum Center and Television City on Manhattan's West Side, and to constrain otherwise the locational choice of capital. The other type is more positive in that it offers alternatives to private-sector market activity. Here our discussion has centered on innovative ways in which communities are pursuing development based on public and third-sector initiatives.

Collective action results when people who share common interests act together. It requires expenditure of time and resources in coordination—finding others with the same interests, communicating with them, and gathering the information on which to base the action.[12] The costs and difficulty of coordination favor smaller rather than larger groups. Larger groups typically get their financial support through continual fund-raising, and, if made up of the relatively poor, by many small material contributions and voluntary commitments of time. Organizing for collective action means defining the group that will benefit, establishing the importance of the benefit clearly enough so that resources will flow to the project despite its uncertainty or the group's general lack of material resources, and overcoming the problem of the group's size through a local focus.

Community-based collective action frequently involves choices over public or collective goods that can be encumbered with the "free-rider" problem. A public good such as a park (fire protection and national defense are other textbook examples) can be consumed by one person without precluding consumption by another. The "free rider," embued with individualistic patterns of thought and the values of the economic man or woman of neoclassical economics, reasons that contributing to creation of the park is not a "rational" free choice, since he or she can use the public good once others pay for it. Even though the use of the park would benefit these individuals, they reason that it serves them best to act disinterested, hoping that others will

[12] For a summary of arguments on barriers to collective action, generally in capitalist democracies and in the United States in particular, see Cohen and Rogers, *On Democracy*, chap. 3. Fuller analysis is provided in Adam Przeworski and Michael Wallerstein, "The Structure of Class Conflict in Democratic Capitalist Societies," *American Political Science Review* 76 (1982), 215–38. Economic constraints to collective action are discussed in Charles E. Lindblom, *Politics and Markets: The World's Political-Economic Systems* (New York, 1977), and Mancur Olson, *The Logic of Collective Action: Public Goods and the Theory of Groups* (Cambridge, Mass., 1965).

pay for its creation. Collective action is also hindered when people count their contribution as a cost, but there is some uncertainty as to whether an equal benefit will be received, either because the collective goal may never be realized or because the individual will choose not to partake of it. In a relatively affluent and privatized economy, a likely individualistic escape from these dilemmas is to opt for personal or private solutions—parks are less desirable to those who own vacation homes or homes with pleasant yards. The calculating individual will then rationally oppose creation of public goods or will favor those that fit their pattern of consumption, such as better roads for the owners of automobiles rather than improved railroad lines. Although the behavior of the rational self-seeker posited in the free rider problem is common in our society, it is not universal or always dominant. People can see means of self-expression and growth in working with others, or they can feel an obligation to contribute to the general welfare in order to count themselves good citizens.

This study has been based on the premise that people's involvement as citizens is most likely to be revitalized and remain high to the extent that they have more, rather than fewer, opportunities and incentives to be a part of the decision-making process at the local level of governance. Elements of this argument have been made—and made well—by many authors. More remains to be said. The two forms of development we have described—economic and political—are closely related. One can retard the other, but the two can work together to qualitatively change both process and outcome. Together they can challenge the interests of those whose primary concern is their private accumulation of capital, and they can change our ways of conducting public life.

Local Action: Reform in a Global Context

Community-based action can serve as a vehicle for citizen participation and more meaningful community life, but it is also attractive for reasons involving broader strategies for social change. The issue of more broadly defined social change brings us to the paradox of local action in an increasingly integrated world, one in which the nation state and groups of nations have grown in importance relative to local units of governance. It also leads us to discussion of the future course of political development in the United States.

We have argued that poor communities remain poor because surplus is drained from them, limiting their basis for development. There are communities in which little market-based productive activity takes place, but they are retirement villages or quintessential bedroom communities. Surplus is generated in most communities. The logic of the system dictates that surplus is then transferred to financial centers, corporate accounts, and stockholders' portfolios. It only comes back if conditions are right to make a good return on new investment (extracting more surplus) or if the poor community begins to attract wealthy residents (unlikely). However, accepted rules of the game have meant that communities could only take action within narrowly defined parameters. The active agents for economic development are preeminently those of the private sector. Public and quasi-public activity is assigned a secondary role, one geared to attracting and pleasing capital or doing without it. What better world for capital? No matter how ugly or unseemly, it is assured numerous suitors. Part of the pleasure of capital ownership is a world of competitors for one's favors.

Reforms can help to ameliorate economic, social, and political underdevelopment resulting from this system of production and distribution. Although we accept the argument that redistributive reform is a reasonable course to pursue—essentially that it combines capitalism's ability to deliver the goods with a rounding-off of its rough edges by reform and regulation—we find reform strategies alone insufficiently forward-looking. Capitalism takes many shapes, from emphasis on markets in the mixed economy of the United States to the extensively regulated and negotiated Swedish version to the authoritarian South Korean form. The problem is that each of them continues to reproduce a world in which private accumulation and power are derived from ownership of means of production. To cast the future in terms of democracy and equality, capital must be constrained to meet social needs in the short run and eliminated as a basis of power in the long run. The only logical means to that end is consciously to bring increasing amounts of social surplus under democratic, public control *before* it reinforces the strength of the dominant few.

Why then concentrate on the local level of activity in society? Earlier we explained some positive reasons for doing so. Some are less positive. So much of the literature on community-based activity has ignored analysis of the way in which capitalism works. The national political arena in recent decades has hardly seemed fruitful. Although important exceptions exist, in general political and economic outcomes of the period have been regressive. Much positive political action and many innovative economic experiments have taken place at the local level, and those attempts are good news, but more is needed.

Capitalism's global competition has made the nation state an ever more central site of social and economic policy-making. National and international arenas increasingly form the context and the limits and opportunities for local activity, for better or worse. Capital will fight for its interests locally and will continue to demand freedom of action in the domestic realm in order to do the best it can "for the country" in international competition. Communities have extensive experience with these arguments in local labor-management disputes over wages and working conditions, environmental regulation, and corporate need for tax concessions. The same conflicts occur at the state and national levels. As concentration and centralization of capital continue, state and local constraints, regulation, and opposition become more costly for capital to monitor, meet, or overcome. The struggle played out in the integration of Europe will surely have its American (Canadian and U.S., and perhaps soon Mexican) counterparts as capital seeks further "rationalization." For the United States, uniform federal regulations have and will continue to be capital's favorite. Capital's use of the state in increasingly instrumental ways and communities increasingly in conflict with such a state are not difficult to imagine.

We want to encourage thinking about how the state itself might be restructured in progressive ways. The necessarily limited concern here is for the impact that community-based citizen pressure may have: how it can bring local communities and community-based groups more fully into roles of shaping policy, enforcing regulation, and generally exercising power.

As the nature of industrial production has changed, large firms have been forced to adopt more flexible management systems such as team concepts of work, de-emphasized hierarchy, and limited forms of workers' participation in management. Fred Block argues that states too will have to adapt to more rapid social and economic change by adopting new organizational forms and operating procedures, and this could open the possibility of debureaucratization of the state. The state will be driven to improve lateral coordination (compared to cumbersome communication up and down bureaucratic organizations), motivate lower-level employees, and enable its branches to take wider initiative in responding to demands. A key element of such a change would be a shift from procedural to substantive forms of regulation. Block offers an example of substantive regulation drawn from emerging Scandinavian practice in workplace health and safety, and argues that it could be extended to areas such as environmental regulation or transportation planning. Rather than limiting emission levels of specific pollutants, it would specify the goal of an increasingly clean environment. And rather than build a large bureaucratic enforcement agency, it would expand the role for nonstate actors in the form of local monitoring and planning committees. The state would support and empower these groups and work with them. Together their use of power would be constrained by the need to present evidence to a judicial body before invoking last-resort legal sanctions. Short of sanctions, agents of the state would strengthen community groups in their negotiation with capital.[13]

Closer to home, the Act 200 Growth Management legislation in Vermont contains elements of this model. Without arguing that the state should or will be less important a coordinating institution, the law empowers citizens to play a more active role in public life. How this law will work in practice and whose interests will ultimately be served remain to be seen. The law has drawn opposition from those defending both local sovereignty and the rights of capital. However, with state resources funneled to citizen groups working on alternative plans, Act 200 has the potential to develop a counterforce to developers' influence on local communities in Vermont. As a more general model, it calls attention to the need for state assistance in developing expertise and support systems for local governance.

We have drawn our argument from several sources. First, although critical of some aspects of left populist thinking, we share its commitment to the struggle for empowerment. Communities must be able to plan for and take action to shape their futures. Second, issues of process and equity are at the heart of these struggles, and we agree with the new left's commitment to participatory democracy in them. Empowerment does not mean empowering a few, but empowering all, and enriching their lives in the process.

[13] Block, *Revising State Theory;* the argument for state debureaucratization can be found on pp. 29–33. Block relies heavily on the impact of "postindustrial" transitions in society to reshape state power, including who will have it.

Third, we have shaped our analysis of economic development using a Marxist framework. Other economic analyses might be used to reach some of the same conclusions, but they would not provide insight into issues of class and power. Not only orthodox economists ignore these issues. New-age spiritualists pretend that conflict can be dispensed with by higher stages of consciousness, and "post-Marxists," in their rush to distance themselves from economic determinism, tend to throw out the complex but essential issues of class and exploitation.[14] Social movements are often analysed in the context of a renewal of liberal, pluralist politics within the existing social order; little thought is given to how they could affect relationships of class and power or how they fail to do so. Without maintaining a clear sense of how a less industrial and more service-based—but still capitalist—economy functions, creating alternatives is that much more difficult.

Clearly, we have adopted in our work a relatively optimistic conception of communities. Our fieldwork put us in touch with communities that are changing in progressive ways. What captured our attention was the process of communities working to redefine themselves. In the most dramatic cases they are shedding parts of their tradition—those based on private monopolies of resource and wealth-holding, or racism and sexism, or environmental degradation—and creating new grounds for fuller, more democratic communities. We conclude with a brief investigation of the nature of this activity and the possibility of its integration into a broader strategy for change.

Social Change

Progressive community-based politics in this country results from a potent mix of activity. One part of it can be labeled instrumental. It is the difficult, time- and resource-consuming march through established institutions of governance, often appearing in the world of electoral politics, including building coalitions to win seats on city councils in places like Berkeley, Santa Monica, and Burlington. Gains in this arena can lead to important reforms, such as improved public

[14] This problem is reflected in Ernesto Laclau and Chantal Mouffe, *Hegemony and Socialist Strategy: Towards a Radical-Democratic Politics* (London, 1985). A trenchant critique of an analysis that turns politics into discourse can be found in Ellen Meiksins Wood, *The Retreat from Class: A New "True" Socialism* (London, 1986).

transit or tenants' rights ordinances with teeth. The instrumental realm also includes building institutions in the form of community development corporations and credit unions. To survive and deliver resources or services to their community, these organizations must function within the rules of the established order. They can do so with positive, politically progressive results.

The other realm of activity, often called prefigurative, is more volatile and involves popular mobilization. Wedded to a world of upheaval, confrontation, and insurgency,[15] it is free—for a while at least—of most institutional constraints. It is prefigurative at the level of community when it proposes alternatives to corporate liberal hegemony. Demands for more complete local governance can run counter to corporate concern for uniform markets and regulation; calls for expanded participation challenge the constrained world of local legislative and executive process and power; protesting plant closings by occupying factories and offices calls into question corporate control of means of production and jobs; noisy demonstrations at public meetings can win resources for improving public services in poor neighborhoods or for environmental protection. This activity takes place in the realm of civil society, even while it can play a role in reshaping state policy.

The U.S. labor movement has been mired in the instrumental realm for decades. The business unionism of the post-war years has been predicated on playing within the rules as defined in the Wagner Act and further constrained by Taft-Hartley. For all its positive outcomes for labor, the Wagner Act was a form of regulation. It effectively severed the prefigurative element of the movement from increasingly centralized and bureaucratic official structure and process. The historically narrow focus of twentieth-century organized labor, first on skilled labor, then on industrial workers, made such an outcome more likely. It kept this movement from including a broader mix of workers in its organizing campaigns and membership. Domestic labor, farm labor, part-time, and service sector work were largely ignored. Con-

[15] See Carl Boggs, *Social Movements and Political Power: Emerging Forms of Radicalism in the West* (Philadelphia, 1986), chaps. 4 and 6. Boggs captures some of the historical texture of this activity in his description of it as "dialectical interplay between subversive impulses and existing traditions, between creative intervention and social immediacy, between the old and the new" (p. 165). For an insightful investigation of the way in which protest movements effect public policy, see Sidney Tarrow, "Struggling to Reform: Social Movements and Policy Change during Cycles of Protest," Western Societies Program Occasional Paper No. 15, Center for International Studies, Cornell University (Ithaca, n.d.).

tentious issues of race and gender were thus avoided, but so too was the opportunity for organized labor to keep itself vital. Labor's support for and work with the civil rights and women's movements could have strengthened those movements and broadened labor's base of support; upheaval and confrontation could have provided a basis for alternative strategy and action prior to the concessionary bargaining of the 1980s. After World War II the U.S. labor movement learned its instrumental role well. Today it is faced with the tasks of regaining its prefigurative character and redefining its role as an agent of progressive change.[16]

Instrumental and prefigurative elements of social transformation are important to understanding community-based activity. Earlier we discussed the distinction between alternative institutions, those willing to be different quietly, and oppositional institutions, those carrying on their affairs but also committed to changing the world in their image. Most of the alternative institutions that we have described reside, however uncomfortably, in the instrumental realm. Oppositional organizations are significant (and vulnerable) because they choose to exist as prefigurative institutions as well. Their terrain of operation is both civil society and the established order of the economy or state. Both realms are legitimate arenas of activity for change; both forms of organization are essential to carrying it on.

Can local action for social change be linked to national activity to encourage more dramatic change? We believe important possibilities exist for effective linkages and for the pressing need to continue conceptual work to sort them out.[17] The wedding of conventional instrumental political activity and popular mobilization for progressive community-based change is a pattern that is familiar at the national level. The civil rights movement made what gains it did because of

[16] The current shape of American labor and the history that led to its condition are evaluated in Mike Davis, *Prisoners of the American Dream* (London, 1986); Michael Goldfield, *The Decline of Organized Labor in the United States* (Chicago, 1986); and Kim Moody, *An Injury to All: The Decline of American Unionism* (London, 1989). A critical review of Moody's book elaborates some of the negative implications of the narrow model of industrial unionism adopted by U.S. labor; see Dana Frank, "Labor's Decline," *Monthly Review* 41 (October 1989), 48–55.

[17] Our thinking on this issue has been influenced by Rowbotham, Segal, and Wainwright, *Beyond the Fragments,* and by Raymond Williams in much of his writing. The editorial introduction to a recent *New Left Review* identified one important task in the work when it argued for identifying "new, more adequate and effective forms of anti-capitalist 'general interest' which will be something more than the sum of particular anti-capitalist movements" ("Themes," *New Left Review* No. 180 [March/April 1990], 3).

the galvanizing impact of public insurgency combined with the tough work of local electoral politics, voter registration, and legislative give-and-take. Popular opinion seems to reflect changing consciousness about women's rights, but it will take renewed activity on the streets and in statehouses and Congress before legislation assuring equal rights for women is enacted. Passage of national legislation cannot end racism or sexism, but it provides another base from which to fight. Finally, the communities where we live are where new social relations must be created to overcome the vices of racism and sexism. Shaping new social relations takes place in the realm of civil society. Consciousness matters, and so does more conventional politics.

This discussion leads inexorably into the thicket of new models of social change that address nation and community and of oppositional politics and social movements. Oppositional political activity is enormously difficult to sustain; it is constantly at risk of being either marginalized or assimilated. Social movements are frequently ambiguous politically, narrowly focused, and made up of members who are dispersed geographically. By nature they tend to lack organizational structure and an ongoing role as strategic players in the political arena. But some of these characteristics can be advantageous as well, for social movements can be powerful destabilizers of business (or politics) as usual. As Carl Boggs has argued, social movements have the "subversive potential" to reach into the cracks in bourgeois hegemony and call into question the ideologies that legitimate existing power structures.[18] At the institutional center of the power structure are corporations and the state and their parallel supporting institutions such as political parties. One or more new political organizations will have to be created, or an existing one transformed, in order to provide the instrumental vehicle needed to sustain a cohesive challenge to the corporate liberal world. Institution-building with some measure of continuity and stability is essential, as is the ability to mobilize people and their resources. Obstacles here include the normal co-optation of everyday political activity and legal and institutional barriers to overcoming the Coke-or-Pepsi world of two-party politics in the United States.[19] Work must proceed on these vexing questions; we have no easy answers for them.

[18] Boggs, *Social Movements and Political Power*, pp. 242–43.

[19] Social movements are not immune from co-optation either. See the often cited intro-

Populist and Green movements in community-based political activity attempt to reframe the question of progressive politics by confronting not simply capital, but state power as well. However, what sometimes emerges is an anti-statist model of social change with little content beyond localism. Civil society becomes all, and the combined power of the state and capital are supposed to somehow evaporate from life. Since that outcome is unlikely, these approaches can lead to forms of local isolationism and ultimately to a politics of simple self-help.

Many thoughtful strategists and activists are wrestling with another model for change. It recognizes many of the implications of a global system of production under the control of capital, and it appraises state activity and power in a different light. Although its vision for the future might include a dramatically less significant state, it counts the state as a locus of power, as an arena worth fighting in and for. Underlying this conceptual approach to community-based politics is an important effort to understand how activity at the level of the state and at the level of civil society can be interwoven. In discussing the ways in which institutional politics and grass-roots activism work in unison, Ralph Miliband describes a state where some progressive gains have been won. Popular support comes from polls, from political parties, and from formal organizations such as trade unions. However, sustaining momentum, overcoming establishment power, and—we would argue—defining the nature of changes worth fighting for require more than politics as usual. Traditional political activity must be reinforced by a larger force in the form of "a flexible and complex network of organs of popular participation operating throughout civil society, and intended *not* to *replace* the state, but to complement it."[20] Together these forms of political and social mobilization win, safeguard, and go on to win more social justice.

This brief sketch points to a means by which some of the usual barriers to social change can be overcome without endlessly debating revolutions that are not on the horizon or turning inward in despair of achieving any change. It recognizes the potential for a rich, less constrained practice of politics, one that could incorporate cultural

---

duction to Frances Fox Piven and Richard Cloward, *Poor People's Movements: How They Succeed and Why They Fail* (New York, 1979).

[20] Ralph Miliband, *Marxism and Politics* (New York, 1977) p. 188 (emphasis in original).

and ideological imperatives of social movements with an assault on established institutional bases of power. And it is a strategy that makes possible fruitful interweaving of local initiatives, grass-roots activism, and politics at the level of the state. The achievements of groups in diverse communities across this country and in many other lands provide instruction and inspiration in meeting this challenge. There are threads of a future here; the weaving awaits us.

Selected Bibliography

Aglietta, Michel. *A Theory of Capitalist Regulation.* London: New Left Books, 1979.

Albelda, Randy, Christopher Gunn, and William Waller, eds. *Alternatives to Economic Orthodoxy: A Reader in Political Economy.* Armonk, N.Y.: M. E. Sharpe, 1987.

Alford, Robert R., and Roger Friedland. *Powers of Theory: Capitalism, the State, and Democracy.* New York: Cambridge University Press, 1985.

Alperovitz, Gar, and Jeff Faux. *Rebuilding America.* New York: Pantheon, 1984.

Baran, Paul A., and Paul M. Sweezy. *Monopoly Capital: An Essay on the American Economic and Social Order.* New York: Monthly Review Press, 1966.

Barber, Benjamin. *Strong Democracy: Participatory Politics for a New Age.* Berkeley: University of California Press, 1984.

Barrett, Michèle. *Women's Oppression Today.* 2d. ed. London: Verso, 1980.

Bartlett, Randall. *Economic Foundations of Political Power.* New York: Free Press, 1973.

Baumol, William J., and Alan S. Blinder. *Economics: Principles and Policy.* 3d ed. San Diego: Harcourt Brace Jovanovich, 1985.

Bell, Clive, Peter Hazell, and Roger Slade. *Project Evaluation in Regional Perspective.* Baltimore, Md.: Johns Hopkins University Press, 1982.

Bellah, Robert N., et al. *Habits of the Heart: Individualism and Commitment in American Life.* Berkeley: University of California Press, 1985.

Bergman, Edward M., ed. *Local Economies in Transition: Policy Realities and Development Potentials.* Durham, N.C.: Duke University Press, 1986.

Berman, Katrina V. *Worker-Owned Plywood Firms: An Economic Analysis.* Pullman: Washington State University Press, 1967.

Berndt, Harry E. *New Rulers in the Ghetto: The CDC and Urban Poverty.* Westport, Conn.: Greenwood Press, 1977.

Birnbaum, Norman. *The Radical Renewal: The Politics of Ideas in Modern America.* New York: Pantheon, 1988.

Blaug, Mark. *Economic Theory in Retrospect.* 3d ed. New York: Cambridge University Press, 1978.

Block, Fred L. *Revising State Theory: Essays in Politics and Postindustrialism.* Philadelphia: Temple University Press, 1987.

Bluestone, Barry, and Bennett Harrison. *The Deindustrialization of America.* New York: Basic, 1982.

Boggs, Carl. *Social Movements and Political Power: Emerging Forms of Radicalism in the West.* Philadelphia: Temple University Press, 1986.

Bookchin, Murray. *Remaking Society.* Montreal: Black Rose Books, 1989.

——. *Toward an Ecological Society.* Montreal: Black Rose Books, 1980.

Bowles, Samuel, and Herbert Gintis. *Democracy and Capitalism: Property, Community, and the Contradictions of Modern Social Thought.* New York: Basic, 1986.

——. *Schooling in Capitalist America.* New York: Basic, 1976.

Bowles, Samuel, David Gordon, and Thomas Weisskopf. *Beyond the Wasteland: A Democratic Alternative to Economic Decline.* New York: Doubleday, 1983.

Boyte, Harry C. *Backyard Revolution: Understanding the New Citizen Movement.* Philadelphia: Temple University Press, 1980.

——. *Community Is Possible: Repairing America's Roots.* New York: Harper and Row, 1984.

Boyte, Harry C., Heather Booth, and Steve Max. *Citizen Action and the New American Populism.* Philadelphia: Temple University Press, 1986.

Bratt, Rachel G., Chester Hartman, and Ann Meyerson, eds. *Critical Perspectives on Housing.* Philadelphia: Temple University Press, 1986.

Brecher, Jeremy, and Timothy Costello. *Building Bridges: The Emerging Grassroots Coalition of Labor and Community.* New York: Monthly Review Press, 1990.

Bruyn, Severyn T., and James Meehan, eds. *Beyond the Market and the State: New Directions in Community Development.* Philadelphia: Temple University Press, 1987.

Burnham, Walter D. *The Current Crisis in American Politics.* New York: Oxford University Press, 1982.

Caja Laboral Popular. *Annual Report 1987.* Guipuzcoa, Spain: Caja Laboral Popular, 1988.

——. *The Mondragon Experiment.* Guipuzcoa, Spain: Caja Laboral Popular, 1987.

Carnoy, Martin. *The State and Political Theory.* Princeton, N.J.: Princeton University Press, 1984.

Carnoy, Martin, and Derek Shearer. *Economic Democracy: The Challenge of the 1980s.* Armonk, N.Y.: M. E. Sharpe, 1980.

Carnoy, Martin, Derek Shearer, and Russell Rumberger. *A New Social Contract.* New York: Harper and Row, 1983.

Case, John, and Rosemary Taylor, eds. *Co-ops, Communes and Collectives.* New York: Pantheon, 1979.

Castells, Manuel. *The City and the Grassroots.* Berkeley: University of California Press, 1983.

——. *City, Class, and Power.* New York: St. Martin's, 1979.

——. *The Urban Question: A Marxist Approach*. Cambridge, Mass.: MIT Press, 1977.

Cherry, Robert, et al., eds. *The Imperiled Economy, Book I: Macro Economics from a Left Perspective*. New York: Union for Radical Political Economy, 1987.

Clavel, Pierre. *The Progressive City: Planning and Participation 1969–1984*. New Brunswick, N.J.: Rutgers University Press, 1986.

Clotfelter, Charles T., and Phillip J. Cook. *Selling Hope: State Lotteries in America*. Cambridge, Mass.: Harvard University Press, 1989.

Cluster, Dick, et al. *The Right to Housing: A Blueprint for Housing the Nation*. Washington, D.C.: Institute for Policy Studies, 1989.

Cohen, Joshua, and Joel Rogers. *On Democracy: Toward a Transformation of American Society*. New York: Penguin, 1983.

Crozier, Michael J., Samuel P. Huntington, and Joji Watanuki. *The Crisis of Democracy: Report on the Governability of Democracies to the Trilateral Commission*. New York: New York University Press, 1975.

Dahl, Robert A. *Democracy and Its Critics*. New Haven, Conn.: Yale University Press, 1989.

Davis, Mike. *Prisoners of the American Dream*. London: Verso, 1986.

Delgado, Gary. *Organizing the Movement: The Roots and Growth of Acorn*. Philadelphia: Temple University Press, 1986.

Downs, Anthony. *An Economic Theory of Democracy*. New York: Harper and Row, 1957.

Du Boff, Richard B. *Accumulation and Power: An Economic History of the United States*. Armonk, N.Y.: M. E. Sharpe, 1989.

Fainstein, Susan S., et al. rev. ed. *Restructuring the City: The Political Economy of Urban Redevelopment*. New York: Longman, 1986.

Ferguson, Thomas, and Joel Rogers, eds. *The Hidden Election: Politics and Economics in the 1980 Presidential Campaign*. New York: Pantheon, 1981.

——. *The Political Economy*. Armonk, N.Y.: M. E. Sharpe, 1984.

Flacks, Richard. *Making History: The American Left and the American Mind*. New York: Columbia University Press, 1988.

Foley, Duncan. *Understanding Capital: Marx's Economic Theory*. Cambridge, Mass.: Harvard University Press, 1986.

Forester, John. *Planning in the Face of Power*. Berkeley: University of California Press, 1989.

Foster, John Bellamy. *The Theory of Monopoly Capitalism*. New York: Monthly Review Press, 1986.

Friedmann, John. *Knowledge and Action: Mapping the Planning Theory Domain*. Princeton, N.J.: Princeton University Press, 1987.

Gaventa, John. *Power and Powerlessness: Quiescence and Rebellion in an Appalachian Valley*. Urbana: University of Illinois Press, 1980.

Gilderbloom, John I., et al. *Rent Control: A Sourcebook*. Santa Barbara, Calif.: Foundation for National Progress, 1981.

Goldfield, Michael. *The Decline of Organized Labor in the United States*. Chicago: University of Chicago Press, 1986.

Goodman, Robert. *The Last Entrepreneurs*. Boston: South End Press, 1979.

Goodwyn, Lawrence. *The Populist Moment.* New York: Oxford University Press, 1978.

Gordon, David M., Richard Edwards, and Michael Reich. *Segmented Work, Divided Workers.* New York: Cambridge University Press, 1982.

Greenberg, Edward S. *Workplace Democracy: The Political Effects of Participation.* Ithaca, N.Y.: Cornell University Press, 1986.

Gunn, Christopher E. *Workers' Self-Management in the United States.* Ithaca, N.Y.: Cornell University Press, 1984.

Gurwitz, Aaron S., and G. Thomas Kingsley. *The Cleveland Metropolitan Economy.* Santa Monica, Calif.: Rand Corporation, 1982.

Gyford, John. *The Politics of Local Socialism.* London: Allen and Unwin, 1985.

Habermas, Jurgen. *Legitimation Crisis.* Trans. Thomas McCarthy. Boston: Beacon, 1975.

Harrison, Bennett. *Urban Economic Development.* Washington, D.C.: Urban Institute, 1974.

Harvey, David. *The Limits to Capital.* Chicago: University of Chicago Press, 1982.

——. *The Urbanization of Capital: Studies in the History and Theory of Capitalist Urbanization.* Baltimore, Md.: Johns Hopkins University Press, 1985.

Henze, Laura J., Edward Kirshner, and Linda Lillow. *An Income and Capital Flow Study of East Oakland, California.* Oakland, Calif.: Community Economics, 1979.

Holland, Stuart. *Capital versus the Regions.* New York: St. Martin's, 1976.

Hunt, E. K. *History of Economic Thought: A Critical Perspective.* Belmont, Calif.: Wadsworth Publishing, 1979.

Jackall, Robert, and Henry M. Levin, eds. *Worker Cooperatives in America.* Berkeley: University of California Press, 1984.

Jacobs, Jane. *Cities and the Wealth of Nations: Principles of Economic Life.* New York: Random House, 1984.

Jencks, Christopher, et al. *Inequality: A Reassessment of the Effect of Family and Schooling in America.* New York: Basic, 1972.

Jessop, Bob. *The Capitalist State: Marxist Theories and Methods.* New York: New York University Press, 1982.

Johnson, David R., John A. Booth, and Richard J. Harris, eds. *The Politics of San Antonio.* Lincoln: University of Nebraska Press, 1983.

Kann, Mark E. *Middle Class Radicalism in Santa Monica.* Philadelphia: Temple University Press, 1986.

Katouzian, Homa. *Ideology and Method in Economics.* New York: New York University Press, 1980.

Katznelson, Ira. *City Trenches: Urban Politics and the Patterning of Class in the United States.* New York: Pantheon, 1981.

Kolko, Joyce. *Restructuring the World Economy.* New York: Pantheon, 1988.

Kotler, Milton. *Neighborhood Government: The Local Foundations of Political Life.* Indianapolis, Ind.: Bobbs-Merrill Co., 1969.

Krumholz, Norman, and John Forester. *Making Equity Planning Work: Leadership in the Public Sector.* Philadelphia: Temple University Press, forthcoming.

Laclau, Ernesto, and Chantal Mouffe. *Hegemony and Socialist Strategy: Towards a Radical-Democratic Politics*. London: Verso, 1985.
Leontief, Wassily. *Input-Output Economics*. 2d ed. New York: Oxford University Press, 1986.
Lindblom, Charles E. *Politics and Markets: The World's Political-Economic Systems*. New York: Basic, 1977.
The Local Economy Inventory Report for Chester, Pennsylvania. 4 vols. New Haven, Conn.: RPM Systems, Inc., 1987.
Love, John F. *McDonald's: Behind the Arches*. New York: Bantam, 1986.
Lynd, Staughton. *The Fight against Shutdowns*. San Pedro, Calif.: Singlejack Books, 1982.
McDonald's Corporation. *1988 Annual Report*. Oak Brook, Ill.: McDonald's Corporation, 1989.
Mackintosh, Maureen, and Hilary Wainwright, eds. *A Taste of Power: The Politics of Local Economics*. London: Verso, 1987.
Mandel, Ernest. *Late Capitalism*. London: Verso, 1975.
Markusen, Ann R. *The Politics of Regions*. Totowa, N.J.: Rowman and Allenheld, 1985.
——. *Regions: The Economics and Politics of Territory*. Totowa, N.J.: Rowman and Littlefield, 1987.
Mexican American Unity Council. *1986 Annual Report*. San Antonio, Tex.: Mexican American Unity Council, 1987.
Miliband, Ralph. *Marxism and Politics*. New York: Oxford University Press, 1977.
Milofsky, Carl, ed. *Community Organizations: Studies in Resource Mobilization and Exchange*. New York: Oxford University Press, 1988.
Mollenkopf, John. *The Contested City*. Princeton: Princeton University Press, 1983.
Moody, Kim. *An Injury to All: The Decline of American Unionism*. London: Verso, 1989.
Morris, David. *The New City States*. Washington, D.C.: Institute for Local Self-Reliance, 1982.
Munkirs, John R. *The Transformation of American Capitalism: From Competitive Market Structures to Centralized Private Sector Planning*. Armonk, N.Y.: M. E. Sharpe, 1985.
Musgrave, Richard A., and Peggy B. Musgrave. *Public Finance in Theory and Practice*. 4th ed. New York: McGraw-Hill, 1984.
National Restaurant Association. *Restaurant Industry Operations Report, 1987*. Philadelphia: Laventhal and Horvath, 1987.
O'Connor, James. *Accumulation Crisis*. New York: Basil Blackwell, 1984.
——. *The Fiscal Crisis of the State*. New York: St. Martin's, 1973.
Odendahl, Teresa. *Charity Begins at Home: Generosity and Self-Interest among the Philanthropic Elite*. New York: Basic, 1990.
Olson, Mancur. *The Logic of Collective Action: Public Goods and the Theory of Groups*. Cambridge, Mass.: Harvard University Press, 1965.
Organization for Economic Cooperation and Development. *National Accounts of OECD Countries, 1964–1981*, vol. 2. Paris: OECD, 1982.

Pateman, Carole. *Participation and Democratic Theory*. Cambridge: Cambridge University Press, 1970.
Pechman, Joseph A. *Who Paid the Taxes, 1966–85*. Washington, D.C.: Brookings Institution, 1985.
Perry, David C., and Alfred J. Watkins, eds. *The Rise of the Sunbelt Cities*. Beverly Hills, Calif.: Sage Publications, 1983.
Phares, Donald. *Who Pays State and Local Taxes?* Cambridge, Mass.: Oelgeschlager, Gunn and Hain, 1980.
Piore, Michael J., and Charles F. Sabel. *The Second Industrial Divide: Possibilities for Prosperity*. New York: Basic, 1984.
Piven, Frances Fox, and Richard Cloward. *Poor People's Movements: How They Succeed and Why They Fail*. New York: Vintage, 1979.
Plotkin, Sidney. *Keep Out: The Struggle for Land Use Control*. Berkeley: University of California Press, 1987.
Przeworski, Adam. *Capitalism and Social Democracy*. New York: Cambridge University Press, 1985.
Rose, Adam, Brandt Stevens, and Gregg Davis. *Natural Resource Policy and Income Distribution*. Baltimore, Md.: Johns Hopkins University Press, 1988.
Routh, Guy. *The Origin of Economic Ideas*. Armonk, N.Y.: M. E. Sharpe, 1975.
Rowbotham, Sheila, Lynne Segal, and Hilary Wainwright. *Beyond the Fragments: Feminism and the Making of Socialism*. London: Verso, 1979.
Stave, Bruce M., ed. *Socialism and the Cities*. Port Washington, N.Y.: Kennikat Press, 1975.
Summers, Gene F., et al. *Industrial Invasion of Non-Metropolitan America: A Quarter Century of Experience*. New York: Praeger, 1976.
Tabb, William K., and Larry Sawers, eds. *Marxism and the Metropolis*. 2d ed. New York: Oxford University Press, 1984.
Taub, Richard P. *Community Capitalism*. Boston: Harvard Business School Press, 1988.
Thomas, Henk, and Chris Logan. *Mondragon: An Economic Analysis*. Boston: Allen and Unwin, 1982.
Tilly, Charles. *From Mobilization to Revolution*. Reading, Mass.: Addison-Wesley, 1978.
U.S. Bureau of the Census. *Statistical Abstract of the United States: 1988*. 108th ed. Washington, D.C.: U.S. Government Printing Office, 1987.
U.S. Congress, Joint Economic Committee. *The Concentration of Wealth in the United States*. Washington, D.C.: J.E.C., 1986.
U.S. Government. *Economic Report of the President*. Washington, D.C.: U.S. Government Printing Office, 1988.
Veblen, Thorstein. *The Instinct of Workmanship*. New York: Macmillan, 1914.
——. *The Theory of the Leisure Class*. New York: Macmillan, 1899.
Walker, Pat, ed. *Between Labor and Capital*. Boston: South End Press, 1979.
Walsh, Annmarie Hauck. *The Public's Business*. Cambridge, Mass.: MIT Press, 1978.
Weisbrod, Burton A. *The Nonprofit Sector*. Cambridge, Mass.: Harvard University Press, 1988.
Whyte, William Foote, and Kathleen King Whyte. *Making Mondragon: The*

Growth and Dynamics of the Worker Cooperative Complex. Ithaca, N.Y.: ILR Press, 1988.
Wolff, Edward N. *Growth, Accumulation and Unproductive Activity: An Analysis of the Postwar U.S. Economy*. New York: Cambridge University Press, 1987.
Wolin, Sheldon. *The Presence of the Past*. Baltimore, Md.: Johns Hopkins University Press, 1989.
Wood, Ellen Meiksins. *The Retreat from Class: A New "True" Socialism*. London: Verso, 1986.
Wright, Erik Olin. *Class, Crisis and the State*. London: Verso, 1978.
——. *Classes*. London: Verso, 1985.
Wright, Erik Olin, et al. *The Debate on Classes*. London: Verso, 1989.
Young, Dennis. *If Not For Profit, For What?* Lexington, Mass.: Lexington Books, 1983.

Index

Library of Congress Cataloging-in-Publication Data

Gunn, Christopher Eaton.
Reclaiming capital : democratic initiatives and community development / Christopher Gunn, Hazel Dayton Gunn.
p. cm.
Includes bibliographical references and index.
ISBN 0-8014-2323-6 (cloth : alk. paper).—ISBN 0-8014-9574-1 (pbk. : alk. paper)
1. Community development—United States. 2. Capitalism—United States. 3. Community power—United States. 4. Community organization—United States. I. Gunn, Hazel Dayton. II. Title.
HN90.C6G86 1991
336'.01473—dc20 90-55725